Computer Guide

Contents

D Lucifer

1. Introduction to Computers

Definition of Computers: -

A computer is an electronic device that processes and stores data performs calculations and executes instructions. Unlike manual tools, computers can perform complex tasks with speed and precision. They are versatile and can handle everything from simple arithmetic to controlling spacecraft.

At its heart, a computer works off of binary code, a group of 0s and 1s that encode instructions and data. There is hardly anything in present society that can function without the help of computers to communicate, solve problems, or enhance efficiency in whatever field in which it may be engaged.

History of Computers: -

Prehistory was marked by manual methods of computing with primitive implements. Here's a historical timeline showing some of the major milestones in the computer evolution process: -

PreMechanical Era: -

Abacus: - One of the earliest computing devices, it dates back to 2400 BCE and was designed mainly for basic arithmetic operations.

Pascaline: - 1642 Blaise Pascal developed a mechanical calculator able to perform addition and subtraction.

Mechanical Era (17th -19th Century): -

Difference Engine: - Charles Babbage constructed the Difference Engine in the 1820s; the mechanical device was intended for calculating polynomial functions.

Analytical Engine: - Later, Babbage designed the Analytical Engine, which also proposed the concept of programmable computers, though never built in his lifetime.

Electromechanical Era (1930s-1940s): -

Zuse Z3: - Konrad Zuse developed it in 1941 and is considered the first programmable digital computer.

ENIAC: - The ENIAC (Electronic Numerical Integrator and Computer) was the first general-purpose electronic computer, built in 1945.

Electronic Era (1940sPresent): -

First Generation (1940s-1950s): - Computers were vacuum tube-based and very large, slow, and energy-intensive.

Second Generation (1950s-1960s): - The invention of the transistor substituted the vacuum tubes in the computer. They were smaller, more reliable computers.

Third Generation (1960s-1970s): - Integrated circuits came in. The size of the computer became even smaller.

Fourth Generation (1970sPresent): - Microprocessors led to the invention of personal computers.

Fifth Generation (Present and Beyond): - Modern computers rely on artificial intelligence, quantum computing, and advanced algorithms.

Significance of Computers in Modern Life

Computers have revolutionized the way we live, work, and interact. Their importance cuts across a range of fields: -

Education: -

Computers are important in education because they provide students with resources and learning platforms that they may not have otherwise accessed. Online courses, virtual classrooms, and educational software enhance learning experiences.

Healthcare: -

Computers are used in healthcare to keep electronic medical records, diagnose diseases, and perform surgeries with robotic assistance. Telemedicine has made health care more accessible.

Communication: -

Computers provide instant communication through emails, video calls, and social media. Zoom and Microsoft Teams are part of everyday personal and professional interactions.

Business and Finance: -

Computers are relied upon for business operations like data management, accounting, and marketing. E-commerce platforms have made it easy for consumers to shop from anywhere.

Science and Research: -

Scientists use computers to simulate scenarios, analyze data, and carry out research in genetics, physics, and climate studies. Supercomputers compute millions of data to answer difficult questions.

Entertainment: -

Computers are the foundation of the entertainment industry, from video editing to gaming, as well as streaming platforms like Netflix. Virtual reality (VR) and augmented reality (AR) improve user experiences.

Transportation: -

In transportation, computers manage traffic systems, design vehicles, and enable navigation through GPS. Autonomous vehicles rely heavily on computer algorithms.

Government and Public Services

Governments use computers to maintain records, conduct elections, and deliver public services efficiently. Digital platforms simplify interactions between citizens and authorities.

Overview of the Book's Contents: -

This book provides an introduction to the principles of computers and guides us through the different topics in an orderly manner. The chapters are comprehensive but simple enough to enable both beginners and those desirous of improving their understanding.

Introduction to Computers: -

Defines what a computer is, and traces its history, and importance.

Hardware and Software: - Defines physical and digital components of the computer.

Number Systems and Logic Gates: - Introduces the building blocks of computing.

Operating Systems: - Explains how operating systems work and why they are important.

Networking: - Explains how computers communicate and share resources.

Storage and Databases: - Focuses on data storage and management.

Cybersecurity: - Emphasizes the need to protect data and devices.

Programming Basics: - Introduces coding and algorithms.

Microsoft Office and Productivity Tools: - Teaches practical skills for using office software.

Advanced Topics: - Explores the newer technologies, including cloud computing and AI.

Computers have extraordinarily changed human life, making them an important tool for most tasks. Their basic knowledge is no longer a skill but rather a necessity in today's digital world. This book serves as a foundation for learning about computers, hence making readers confidently explore new advanced concepts and technologies.

2. Computer Fundamentals and Terminologies

Based on the above discussion of what a computer is and its role in modern life, this chapter delves deeper into the fundamental components of a computer and the essential terms every user should understand. These basics are the building blocks for exploring more advanced topics later in the book.

Basic Computer Components: - Hardware and Software

In order to understand how a computer works, it is important to recognize the two main parts that make up a computer: hardware and software.

1. Hardware

Hardware means the physical parts of the computer that you can see and touch. These components do the work and interact with the software.

The primary hardware components are: -

Input Devices: -

Devices like keyboards, mice, scanners, and webcams enable users to input data and commands into the computer.

Example: - A keyboard is used to input text and a mouse to navigate through the screen and click on items.

Output Devices: -

These components display or convey the results of the computer's processing to the user. Examples include monitors, printers, and speakers.

Example: - A monitor displays text and graphics while speakers output sound.

Processing Unit: -

Central Processing Unit (CPU): - The "brain" of the computer, the CPU executes instructions, performs calculations, and controls data.

Graphics Processing Unit (GPU): - Specialized for rendering images, videos, and animations.

Storage Devices: -

Primary Storage: - Includes RAM (Random Access Memory), which is volatile and temporarily stores data for quick access.

Secondary Storage: - Includes hard drives (HDDs), solid-state drives (SSDs), and USB drives for long-term data storage.

Motherboard: -

The main circuit board ties all the hardware components together and allows them to communicate with one another.

Power Supply Unit (PSU): -

Converts electricity from an outlet into usable power for the computer's components.

2. Software

Software is the set of instructions, programs, or data a computer follows to perform a specific task. Software is intangible and works hand in hand with hardware. It can be divided into two main categories: -

System Software: -

Software that supervises the hardware and facilitates the running of other software applications.

Application: -

Specialized application programs. The programs intended to achieve particular tasks or operations.

These include:

Example -: Word writing and browsing software is Microsoft Word and Google Chrome, respectively.

Utility: -

Programs used in managing, assessing, and adjusting a computer

Example-: Antivirus software as well as cleaning tools in disk cleanup.

To move around the world of computers, it's important to understand some basic terminologies. Here are some key terms and their meanings: -

Bit and Byte: -

A bit is the smallest unit of data in a computer represented as 0 or 1.

A byte is composed of 8 bits and is used to represent characters such as letters and numbers.

Operating System (OS): -

The software that manages computer hardware and software resources.

Example: - Windows 10, macOS Ventura.

CPU or "brain" of a computer: It is meant to execute instructions.

Memory: - Temporary (RAM) and permanent (Storage Drives) where the data is held.

File: - A group of data or information kept electronically, like a document an image, or a video.

Network: - Interconnected computers and devices meant to share data and other resources.

Example: -The internet is a network connecting the whole world.

Cloud Computing: -

Storing and accessing data and programs over the internet instead of on a local hard drive.

Virus and Malware: -

Malicious software designed to disrupt, damage, or gain unauthorized access to systems.

Firewall: -

A security system that monitors and controls incoming and outgoing network traffic.

Overview of Computer Processes and Operations

Computers perform tasks through a series of operations and processes. Here's a simplified explanation: -

1. Input Processing Output Cycle

The three main steps involved in the computer's basic operation include: -

Input: The users provide data by the input devices.

Example: Typing on the keyboard or clicking with the mouse.

Processing: -

The CPU processes the data inputted into it, involving calculations, execution of instructions, and decisions made from the programmed logic.

Example: -A spreadsheet program that will calculate the totals.

Output: -The processed data is then presented to the user by the output device.

Example: - Monitor displaying a completed document.

2. Data Storage

A computer stores data in RAM as a temporary storage system during its processing and also permanently on hard drives or SSDs. The data is read-only when needed to serve the operating process.

3. Executing Programs

The moment a user is running his program, then the CPU fetches instructions from software, decodes them, and executes them sequentially. That is called the fetch-decode execute cycle.

4. Networking and Communication

In networked environments, computers communicate by sending and receiving data packets. This is ensured by protocols like TCP/IP so that the data reaches its destination precisely.

5. Security Operations

Today's computers are always running some background processes to secure data and systems from threats. Such operations include antivirus scans, firewall monitoring, and encryption.

The basics of computer hardware, software, and processes form the foundation for learning more complex topics. If one understands these core concepts, he or she will be able to approach technology with confidence and appreciate it more fully.

3. Computer Hardware

Hardware refers to the physical and tangible part of the computer system. The part is composed of various components which work together to perform several functions including processing data, storing information, and interacting with the user. In this module, we will examine in detail the major hardware elements such as input devices, output devices, storage units, and processing units. Knowing these will make it easier for you to comprehend how a computer works. Input Devices: Input devices allow users to provide data and commands to the computer. They act as a communication bridge between the user and the system.

Following are some commonly used input devices: -

Keyboard: -The most common input device to type text, numbers, and commands. There are two types of keyboards: QWERTY, ergonomic, and mechanical keyboards.

Mouse: - A pointing device used to navigate and interact with graphical user interfaces. There are various types like optical, wireless, and trackball mice.

Scanner: - Converts physical documents or images into digital formats for editing or storage. Microphone: -

Captures audio and converts it into digital signals, enabling voice communication or recording.

Touchscreen: - Input and output functionality combined, where the user interacts directly with the display.

Camera/Webcam: - Captures images or videos for conferencing, photography, or security purposes. Output Devices Output devices display or convey the results of the computer's processing to the user. These devices are crucial for interpreting data and understanding the computer's functions.

Monitor: It gives graphical output, for example, text, images, and video. The type of monitor can be LCD, LED, and OLED monitors. Printer: It converts the digital output to physical paper output. Examples include inkjet, laser, and 3D printers.

Speakers: They create audio outputs that are played to have music, notifications, or even voice communication.

Projector: Project graphical output to a big screen, it is common for classes or presentation use.

Headphones: these can give personalized audio outputs, especially during private listening. Storage devices are responsible for saving data permanently and/or temporarily. Ranges of storage devices include Volatile memory e.g., RAM Non-volatile devices, e.g., Hard disc and USB drive.

Primary Storage RAM (Random Access Memory): - Temporary memory used by the computer to store data currently being processed. Faster than secondary storage but volatile, meaning data is lost when the computer is turned off.

Secondary Storage Hard Disk Drives (HDDs): - Traditional storage devices that use spinning disks to read and write data. They offer large storage capacity at a lower cost but slower compared to SSDs.

Solid-state Drives (SSDs): - Store data in flash memory. Hence, read and write operations occur much faster compared to HDDs. More resistant and energy-friendly but generally expensive.

USB Drives: - External, portable, and compact storage for copying and backup purposes. They are also referred to as pen drives or thumb drives.

Optical Storage CD/DVD/Bluray Discs: Stores data on discs, using laser technology for reading purposes. They are most often used to store media or archives. Cloud Storage The users' data is stored on distant servers that are accessed over the internet.

Examples: Google Drive, Dropbox, OneDrive. Processing Unit The heart of the computer is the processing unit, the part that executes the instruction and computes. Examples: CPU, GPU, and motherboard are included within the processing unit.

1. Central Processing Unit (CPU) The computer's "brain". Carries out instructions, performs arithmetic calculations, and controls tasks. Consists of two major parts: - the Control Unit (CU): - Which controls the flow of data and

instructions in the computer. Arithmetic Logic Unit (ALU): - Carries out mathematical and logical operations. CPUs are differentiated by the number of cores (single-core, dual-core, quad-core, etc.) and clock speed measured in GHz.

2. Graphics Processing Unit (GPU) Specialized processor for rendering graphics, videos, and animations. It is vital for gaming, video editing, and AI applications. Contemporary GPUs also play a part in parallel processing tasks in computing.

3. Motherboard The main circuit board of a computer, linking all the components of a computer, including the CPU, GPU, RAM, and storage devices. It acts as a communication hub that lets data flow between various parts of the computer. This circuit board contains slots for expansion cards, ports for peripherals, and connectors for the power supply.

4. Cooling Systems Maintain optimal temperatures for the CPU and GPU to avoid overheating. Examples: - Fans, heat sinks, liquid cooling systems. How Hardware Works Together Each hardware component plays a specific role, but they work together to get tasks done.

For example: - Input: - A user types a document using a keyboard (input device).

Storage: - The file is stored in an SSD.

Output: - The finished document is displayed on a monitor (output device) or printed. Conclusion Understanding computer hardware is essential to knowing how a computer operates. Each component, from the input devices to the processing unit, plays a crucial role in ensuring that the system functions efficiently. With this knowledge, readers can better appreciate the technology behind modern computing and make informed decisions when using or upgrading their systems.

4. Computer Software

The software is the intangible component of a computer system that gives it its functionality. It is simply a collection of instructions, which guides the hardware in terms of what to do and how to do it. The body of the computer is hardware, and its mind is the software. The main two categories of software are system software and application software. In addition, the opensource software differs from proprietary software.

System Software

System software is the heart of every computer system. It provides an interface between the hardware and the user. System software controls the hardware resources and serves as a basis for the execution of application software.

1. Operating Systems (OS)

An operating system is the most important system software. It deals with the basic functions of the computer, including hardware resource management, communication between software and hardware, and user interface. Some of the most widely used operating systems are: -

Windows: -

Developed by Microsoft, it is one of the most popular operating systems for personal computers.

Known for its user-friendly interface and wide compatibility with software and hardware.

macOS: - It is the operating system Apple uses for Mac computers. Best known for its sleek looks, seamless integration with all other Apple products, and robust performance.

Linux: - It is an opensource operating system that is completely customizable and free to use.

Often used for servers, programming, and educational purposes due to its flexibility and security.

2. Utility Software

Utilities are specialized programs within system software designed to perform specific maintenance tasks. Examples include: -

Antivirus Software: - Protects against malware and viruses.

Disk Cleanup Tools: - Helps free up storage space by removing unnecessary files.

File Management Tools: - Helps to sort, copy, or delete files.

3. Drivers

Drivers are a form of system software that allow the operating system to communicate with hardware devices such as printers, cameras, or graphic cards. Without the proper drivers, these devices may not work.

Application software is designed for specific tasks, which makes it easier for users to accomplish their goals. Unlike system software, application software is useroriented and directly serves the user's needs.

1. Productivity Software

These applications help users perform daily tasks efficiently. Examples include: -

Microsoft Office Suite: -

Includes programs like Word (word processing), Excel (spreadsheets), and PowerPoint (presentations).

Widely used in businesses, schools, and homes.

Google Workspace: -

A cloud-based suite of tools, including Google Docs, Sheets, and Slides, for collaborative work.

2. Web Browsers

Web browsers allow users to access the internet. Popular browsers include: -

Google Chrome: - Known for its speed and extensive library of extensions.

Mozilla Firefox: - Private and secure.

Microsoft Edge: - Integrated with Windows and optimized for performance.

3. Media and Entertainment Software

Applications that cater to creative and leisure activities, such as: -

VLC Media Player: - Free, versatile video and audio player.

Adobe Photoshop: - Professional tool for image editing and graphic design.

Gaming Platforms: - Software such as Steam gives users access to, and the ability to play, video games.

4. Communication Tools “Enable interaction and collaboration, including: - "

Zoom: - Used for video conferencing and virtual meetings.

WhatsApp and Microsoft Teams: - Facilitate instant messaging and collaborative work environments.

Open Source vs. Proprietary Software

This debate between open source and proprietary software usually arises in choosing software for personal or professional use. Both have very distinct characteristics that make them suitable for different purposes.

Opensource Software

Opensource software is freely available to the public. Users can view, modify, and distribute the source code.

Advantages: -

CostEffective: - Most open-source software is free to use.

Customizable: - Users may alter the software to fulfill their specific needs. “

Community Support: - Many open-source projects have lively communities that support and upgrade regularly. “

Examples: -

Linux (operating system). “

LibreOffice (productivity software). “

GIMP (image editing). “

Proprietary Software

Proprietary software is owned by a company or individual. Users buy a license to use it, but they cannot access or modify the source code.

Advantages: -

UserFriendly: - Mostly designed with ease of use in mind.

Dedicated Support: - Offers professional customer support and updates.

Security: - Maintained by the developers, so it remains consistent in performance and less vulnerable.

Examples: -

Microsoft Windows and Office.

Adobe Photoshop.

macOS.

...

How System and Application Software Work Together

System and application software work on interdependence and collaborate to render the computer functional.

For example: -

1. System Software:-The operating system manages the hardware resources to give it a stable platform.

2. Application Software: - Runs on this platform to allow users to perform specific tasks, such as creating documents or browsing the internet.

For example, when using Microsoft Word, the OS allocates memory and processing power to run the application, while Word provides the tools for word processing.

Software is the lifeblood of a computer, which turns a mere hardware into a powerful tool. The knowledge of differences between system software and application software and whether to go for open-source or proprietary software gives a user all the power to take the decision. Through this, readers can learn how computers become more useful and useful in daily life by enhancing their versatility.

5. Number System

A number system is basically an element of computing that essentially establishes a way in which data has been represented, stored and manipulated inside computers. Computers, of course, use varied number systems to perform operations such as calculations, to store information, and consequently communicate. In this part of the chapter, let us know more about the different number systems, how to change one to another, and how important they are for computer users.

Types of Number Systems

There are four main types of number systems used in computing: -

1. Binary Number System (Base2)

The binary number system is the most elementary in computing.

It consists only of two digits:-0 and 1, known as bits.

Computers function based on binary because digital circuits comprehend two states:- on(1) and off (0).

Examples: -

Binary equivalent of decimal 5: - 101

Binary equivalent of decimal 10: - 1010

2. Decimal Number System (Base10)

The decimal system is most widely used by humans in day-to-day calculations.

It comprises ten digits: - 0, 1, 2, 3, 4, 5, 6, 7, 8, 9.

In computing, decimal values are often converted to binary for processing. Examples: - Decimal 5 remains 5 in its own system. Decimal 10 is 10 in this system.

3. Octal Number System (Base8) The octal system uses eight digits: - 0, 1, 2, 3, 4, 5, 6, 7.

It is often used as a shorthand for binary because every three binary digits correspond to one octal digit.

Examples: -

Octal equivalent of binary 110: - 6

Octal equivalent of decimal 10: - 12

4. Hexadecimal Number System (Base16)

The hexadecimal system uses sixteen symbols:-09 and AF, where A=10, B=11, and so on up to F=15. It is frequently used in programming and computing since it makes binary representation much easier (every four binary digits equal one hexadecimal digit). Examples: Hexadecimal equivalent of the binary 1111 - F

Hexadecimal value for decimal 255: - FF

Conversion Between Number Systems

Conversion between number systems is a basic computing skill. Below are the conversion procedures for the most commonly encountered systems: -

1. Decimal to Binary

Divide the decimal number by 2.

Write down the remainder (0 or 1).

Repeat the process with the quotient until it is 0. Write the remainder in reverse order. Example: - Convert 10 (decimal) to binary: - 10 ÷ 2 = 5 remainder 0 5 ÷ 2 = 2 remainder 1 2 ÷ 2 = 1 remainder 0

1 ÷ 2 = 0 remainder 1

Binary: - 1010

2. Decimal to Binary

Multiply each binary digit by 2 raised to the power of its position (from right to left, starting at 0).

Add the results.

Example: - Convert 1010 (binary) to decimal: -

$(1 \times 2^3) + (0 \times 2^2) + (1 \times 2^1) + (0 \times 2^0) = 8 + 0 + 2 + 0 = 10$ (decimal)

3. Decimal to Octal

Divide the decimal number by 8.

Record the remainder.

Repeat until the quotient becomes 0.

Write the remainder in reverse order.

Example: - Convert 65 (decimal) to octal: -

65 ÷ 8 = 8 remainder 1

8 ÷ 8 = 1 remainder 0

1 ÷ 8 = 0 remainder 1

Octal: - 101

4. Octal to Decimal

Multiply each octal digit by 8 raised to the power of its position (from right to left, starting at 0).

Add the results.

Example: - Convert 101 (octal) to decimal: -

$(1 \times 8^2) + (0 \times 8^1) + (1 \times 8^0) = 64 + 0 + 1 = 65$ (decimal)

5. Binary to Hexadecimal

Group binary digits into sets of four (from right).

Replace each group with its corresponding hexadecimal value.

Example: Convert 11110000 from binary to hex:

Group:

1111 and 0000

Hex:

F0

6. Binary Hexadecimal

Convert each hexadecimal digit into its binary equivalent using 4 bits for every one of them.

Example: - Convert A3 (hexadecimal to binary: -

A = 1010, 3 = 0011

Binary: - 10100011

Importance of Number Systems in Computing

Number systems play an important role in computing for the following reasons: -.

1. Data Representation: -

Computers store and process all data in a binary form.

Text, images, as well as videos are encoded into binary for computation purposes.

2. Efficient Processing: -

This is because binary is appropriate for digital circuits since data is represented as a state of being on/off.

Hexadecimal simplifies binary data, making it easier for humans to understand.

3. Networking: -

IP addresses and MAC addresses in computer networks are often represented using decimal, binary, or hexadecimal systems.

4. Programming: -

Programmers use hexadecimal to simplify binary coding and memory addressing.

This will make a person understand the concept of debugging and low-level programming.

5. Storage and Memory: -

The sizes of files, memory, and storage devices are commonly measured in units such as kilobytes (KB), megabytes (MB), and gigabytes (GB) that have a basis in binary.

6. Error Detection: -

Number systems are very important in algorithms that contain error detection and correction, leading to the reliable transmission of data.

Number systems are the foundation of computing. From binary to hexadecimal, each system serves a particular purpose to achieve efficient data representation and processing. Mastery of number systems and conversions enables the user to understand how computers work at their core, and this is a vital subject to be covered by any individual studying computer science or its related fields.

6. Basic Logic Gates

Logic gates are the primary building blocks of digital circuits and computer systems. These perform basic logical functions required for processing data and decision-making within a computer. An understanding of logic gates is essential for anyone who would like to know how computers work, as they constitute the basis of all digital operations.

Introduction to Logic Gates

Logic gates are electronic circuits that perform logical operations on one or more binary inputs to provide one binary output. Each gate has a specific rule based on which it decides the output according to its inputs. These gates work upon binary logic, which means it works with two states only: - 0 (false) and 1 (true).

There are seven fundamental types of logic gates, and every single one performs a different task.

These are: -

AND Gate

OR Gate

NOT Gate

NAND Gate

NOR Gate

XOR Gate

XNOR Gate

Let's study each one in detail.

1. AND Gate

Symbol: - A flat-ended shape with two or more input lines on the left and one output line on the right.

Function: - It gives 1 only when all inputs are 1.

Truth Table: -

Input A\Input B\Output

0\t0\t0

0\t1\t0

1\t0\t0

1\t1\t1

Application: - Used in scenarios where multiple conditions must be met simultaneously. For example, a security system that only unlocks a door if both the correct password and a keycard are provided.

2. OR Gate

Symbol: - A curved shape with two or more input lines on the left and one output line on the right.

Function: - Outputs 1 if at least one input is 1.

Truth Table: -

Input		output
A	B	O
0	0	0
0	1	1
1	0	1
1	1	1

Application: - It is applied wherever any one of the many conditions may cause an action. For instance, if any one of several switches is flipped, then a light is turned on.

3. NOT Gate

Symbol: - A triangle pointing to the right with a small circle at the output representing inversion.

Function: - Outputs the inverse of the input. If the input is 1, the output is 0, and vice versa.

Truth Table: -

Input Output

0 1

1 0

Application: - Used to invert signals, like turning a high signal low or vice versa. Example: In a circuit that should deactivate a device if the condition is not met.

4. NAND Gate

Symbol: - Almost the same as the AND gate except for a small circle drawn at the output.

Function: - The output will be 0 only when all inputs are 1. It is the inverse of the AND gate.

Truth Table: -

Input A\Input B\Output

0\t0\t1

0\t1\t1

1\t0\t1

1\t1\t0

Application: - Used extensively in digital circuits as a universal gate, that is, any other gate can be formed using only NAND gates. For instance, the memory storage elements in computers.

5. NOR Gate

Symbol: - Same as the OR gate but with a small circle at the output.

Function: - Outputs 1 only if all inputs are 0. It is the inverse of the OR gate.

Truth Table: -

Input A\tInput B\tOutput

0\t0\t1

0\t1\t0

1\t0\t0

1\t1\t0

Application:- used in digital circuits where the output needs to be activated only when none of the inputs are activated For example, in alarm systems that activate only when no sensor detects movement.

6. XOR Gate (Exclusive OR)

Symbol: - As that of the OR gate but with an additional curve drawn before the input.

Function: - It gives an output of 1 if any of the two inputs is 1. If both are the same, then the output is 0.

Truth Table: -

Input A	Input B	Output
0	0	0
0	1	1
1	0	1
1	1	0

Application: - Used in the circuit where toggling has to be done, such as digital adders and parity checkers.

7. XNOR Gate (Exclusive NOR)

Symbol: - This gate looks similar to the XOR gate with a small circle at the output.

Function: - Outputs 1 if both inputs are the same. If the inputs are different, the output is 0. It is the inverse of the XOR gate.

Truth Table: -

Input A\tInput B\tOutput

0\t0\t1

0\t1\t0

1\t0\t0

1\t1\t1

Application: - Often used in equality detectors and digital comparators to check if two binary numbers are the same.

Truth Tables and Applications in Computing

A truth table is a mathematical representation table used to determine a logic gate's output based on all possible combinations of its inputs. Truth tables have the importance of designing digital circuits and understanding them. There is a clear and organized manner to show how gates work on various conditions of input.

Sample Example: - Truth Table of an AND Gate

Input A	Input B	Output
0	0	0
0	1	0
1	0	0
1	1	1

By analyzing the truth table, we can understand that the AND gate is going to output a 1 only when both inputs are 1. This will enable engineers to design the circuits that will perform specific logical operations required for computing tasks.

Applications in Computing:

Arithmetic Logic Units (ALUs):

Logic gates are used within ALUs to perform arithmetic operations such as addition, and subtraction, and logical operations such as AND, and OR.

Memory Storage: -

Flipflops and other memory elements in computer RAM use combinations of logic gates to store binary data.

Control Units: -

The control unit of a CPU uses logic gates to decode instructions and manage the flow of data within the computer.

Digital Signal Processing: -

Logic gates help in processing digital signals, enabling functions like filtering, modulation, and error detection.

Real-world Examples of Logic Gates

Logic gates are not just some concepts in books; they find practical usage in various appliances and devices in our lives. Here are some examples in the real world where logic gates play the most crucial role: -

Smartphones: -

Millions of logic gates in smartphones are doing everything starting from touch inputs to app running and communicating.

Home Appliances: -

Logic gates are present in the control of the latest versions of washing machines and microwave ovens while managing settings and operations of different sorts.

Traffic Lights: -

Logic gates govern the timing of traffic lights, which is how they change in a safe and orderly fashion.

Remote Controls: -

Logic gates are responsible for the decoding of signals from remote controls that execute commands such as channel changes or volume changes on televisions and other electronic appliances.

Computers and Laptops: -

Each activity of a computer, including booting up to running an application, depends on logic gates inside the CPU and other components.

Automotive Systems: -

Modern cars use logic gates in their electronic control units (ECUs) to manage engine functions, safety systems, and infotainment features.

Gaming Consoles: -

Gaming consoles use logic gates to handle game logic, graphics rendering, and user inputs, ensuring smooth and responsive gameplay.

Example Scenario: - Traffic Light Control

Consider a traffic light system at an intersection. The logic gates determine when each light (red, yellow, green) should be on or off based on the current state and timing.

For example

An AND gate might ensure that the green light for one direction only turns on if the yellow light for the other direction is off.

A NOT gate could reverse the signal from a sensor detecting traffic, so lights would change only when no car is present.

By making use of combinations of logic gates, the system properly manages the flow of traffic, preventing accidents and reducing congestion.

Logic gates are the basic building blocks of computers and other digital devices that enable them to perform complicated tasks. Understanding the different types of logic gates, how to interpret truth tables, and their real-world applications gives one a good understanding of the inner workings of technology. Whether it is your smartphone, computer, or even the appliances you use daily, logic gates work silently and efficiently to make modern life possible.

7. Operating Systems (OS)

An Operating System, or OS, is perhaps the most basic element in a computer system. It functions as a middleman that bridges between users and their applications on one side, and computer hardware on the other, facilitating the efficient performance of activities. An operating system supervises resources, runs processes, and allows for interaction with users; hence it is one of the very basic parts of modern computing.

An operating system is a category of system software that takes control of computer hardware and software resources. It offers crucial services to computer programs by making sure that hardware elements, such as the CPU, memory, and storage devices, work in harmony.

Without an OS, users would have to interact directly with hardware using cumbersome machine language. The OS makes it easier by offering an environment in which users can run applications without having direct control over the hardware.

Key Features of an Operating System: -

1. Resource Management: - It manages resources, such as CPU time, memory, and storage, for different programs.

2. User Interface: - It gives an interface, either command-line or graphical, to the user for interaction.

3. Program Execution: It enables application execution by managing processes and jobs.

4. Security and Protection: It protects data and system resources from unauthorized access.

Functions of an Operating System

An Operating System performs a number of critical functions that enable a computer to function smoothly: -

1. Process Management

Process management is managing multiple tasks or processes running on a computer. A process is an instance of a program in execution. The OS manages these processes by: -

Scheduling: - Determines which process gets the CPU at any given time.

Multitasking: - Allows multiple processes to run simultaneously by switching between them rapidly.

Interprocess Communication (IPC): - Enables processes to exchange information and coordinate their activities.

Process Synchronization: - It ensures the processes that share resources, do not interfere with other processes.

For instance, the OS ensures that when you stream a video and you are downloading files, two processes share system resources correctly.

2. Memory Management

Memory Management is very important for maximization of the use of Random Access Memory of a computer. The OS manages:

Allocation and Deallocation: Memory to the process and freeing that memory whenever not needed anymore.

Virtual Memory: Providing extended memory that makes some portions of the hard disk used as a type of RAM. In this regard, users can be able to operate applications which consume larger space than that physically presented.

Memory Protection: The situation prevents one process from access in another process' allocated memory while ensuring data integrity and security.

For instance, while using several applications, the OS makes sure each program gets sufficient memory space to operate without interference.

3. I/O Management

The OS regulates the exchange of information between the computer and its I/O devices such as keyboards, mice, printers, and displays. The OS plays a controller's role which has functions to - Communicate to I/O devices -: ensures the exchange of data from the system and I/O devices.

Device Drivers: - Acts as an interpreter between hardware devices and the OS.

Buffering and Caching: - Temporarily stores data to improve the efficiency of I/O operations.

For example, when you print a document, the OS manages the data flow from your computer to the printer.

Types of Operating Systems

There are several types of operating systems, each developed for different needs. These include: -

1. Batch Operating Systems

Batch operating systems were some of the earliest OS types. They process batches of jobs with similar requirements without user interaction. Jobs are collected, grouped, and executed sequentially.

Characteristics: -

No direct user interaction.

Processes jobs in bulk to save time.

Applications: - Used in early computing for tasks like payroll processing or scientific calculations.

Example: - Early IBM mainframe systems.

2. TimeSharing Operating Systems

Time sharing OS permits several users to access a system at the same time by sharing the CPU time with each other. Each user gets a time slice, and thus all the users feel that they have exclusive access.

Characteristics: -

Multiuser capability.

Efficient utilization of CPU.

Applications: - Used in systems where many users require simultaneous access, like university servers.

Example: - UNIX.

3. Distributed Operating Systems

Distributed OS runs across multiple computers connected by a network. It provides an integrated interface as if the system is running on a single machine.

Characteristics: -

Shared resources across systems.

Increased efficiency and reliability.

Applications: - Used in systems requiring high computing power and fault tolerance, such as scientific research.

Example: - Google's cluster of servers.

4. RealTime Operating Systems (RTOS)

RealTime OS is designed for applications that require immediate response to events. These systems rank tasks according to their deadlines.

Characteristics: -

Predictable response times.

High reliability.

Applications: - Used in embedded systems, robotics, and medical devices.

Example: - VxWorks, used in spacecraft systems.

The OS influences the users' interaction with computers significantly. Here is how it makes a difference: -User Experience: An OS that is userfriendly, like Windows or macOS, can make even non-technical users operate a computer without a hitch.

Application Support: The OS is the foundation on which numerous applications run.

Efficiency: An operating system manages the available resources well to ensure seamless multi-tasking and stability of the system.

For instance, an operating system like Android or iOS takes care of the device when you use your smartphone and performs everything from app launch to saving files for smooth functioning and user convenience.

Operating System The Operating System is the foundation of any computer system as it allows hardware and software to function in harmony. This system simplifies the complex process of computing and thus offers users an efficient, secure, and interactive medium to operate. It controls all the processes, memory, and I/O devices along with various types of systems which makes it a key factor of modern technology.

Understanding how operating systems function and their different types helps both users and professionals to see clearer the core of digital systems. As technology develops further, operating systems will still play a very important role in bridging the gap between human interaction and machine operation.

8. Networking Fundamentals

Networking is at the heart of modern-day communication and information sharing. It connects computers and other devices, allowing them to share data and resources seamlessly. Whether it's accessing files, surfing the web, or communicating across borders, networking plays a critical role in making these tasks smooth.

What is Networking?

In simple words, networking refers to the process of connecting several devices such as computers, servers, or printers for the purpose of sharing data, resources, and services. The method of connectivity depends on the type and the purpose of the network as it could be either wired or wireless.

Networking helps individuals and organizations share files and resources such as printers or storage devices and gain access to the internet and cloudbased services.

Use tools like email, video conferencing, and messaging apps to communicate.

Imagine a school where all the students can access shared study materials from a central server. Networking makes this possible by connecting all the computers in the school to the server.

Types of Networks

Networks can be classified according to their size, purpose, and the distance they cover. Here are some common types: -

1. Local Area Network (LAN)

Definition: - LAN is a network that connects devices within a limited area, such as a home, school, or office.

Characteristics: -

Covers a small geographical area.

High speed and reliability.

Use Case: - Sharing files between computers in an office.

2. Wide Area Network (WAN)

Definition: - WAN spans a large geographical area, often connecting multiple smaller networks like LANs.

Characteristics: -

Covers large distances even worldwide.

Usually more slow than LAN as its coverage area is bigger.

Use Case: - Internet is the biggest example of WAN.

3. Metropolitan Area Network (MAN)

Definition: - MAN covers a city or a huge campus.

Characteristics: -

More significant in comparison to LAN but lesser in comparison to WAN

Used to connect various departmental offices of an organization that falls within the city.

Use Case: - Metropolitan area networks for municipal public transport or emergency communications.

4. The Internet

Definition: - The network that links billions of private, public, academic, and business networks worldwide.

Characteristics: -

Decentralized and huge.

Relies on protocols such as TCP/IP to communicate

Use Case: - Reach out to websites, watch streams, or converse on the global network.

. OSI Model and Its 7 Layers

The OSI (Open Systems Interconnection) Model is a conceptual framework that explains how data is transmitted between devices in a network. It is divided into seven layers, each with a specific function: -

1. Physical Layer: -

Deals with the physical connection between devices.

Includes cables, switches, and network interface cards.

Example: - Ethernet cables.

2. Data Link Layer: -

It handles data transfer between adjacent network nodes.

It ensures error-free data transmission.

Example: - MAC (Media Access Control) addresses.

3. Network Layer: -

It is responsible for routing and forwarding data packets.

It uses IP (Internet Protocol) addresses for device identification.

Example: - Routers.

4. Transport Layer: -

Ensures that data is transferred reliably between devices.

It divides data into smaller packets and reconstructs them at the receiving end.

Example: - TCP (Transmission Control Protocol).

5. Session Layer: -

Deals with sessions or connections between devices.

It prevents data from one session from interfering with another.

Example: - Login sessions.

6. Presentation Layer: -

Formats and encrypts data for sending.

Ensures the data is readable to the receiving device.

Example: - Data compression.

7. Application Layer: -

It's the closest layer to the user and provides network services.

It contains all applications like browsers, e-mail, and file transfer tools.

Example: - HTTP (Hypertext Transfer Protocol).

The OSI model is useful for debugging network problems because it will point out which layer has the problem.

IP Addresses and Domains

IP Address

An IP (Internet Protocol) address is a unique address given to each device in a network. It's similar to a mailing address in that it makes sure that data packets reach their intended destination.

Types of IP Addresses:

IPv4

Uses a 32-bit address, such as 192.168.1.1.

IPv6: - Provides a 128-bit address, thus the pool is much larger in comparison.

When you click a site to visit it, it will use your IP to talk to its server

Domain Names

Domain names a readable, and understandable to human beings who can memorize it much easily. Example:-

Domain Name: - `www.google.com`

IP Address: - `142.250.190.78`

The Domain Name System translates domain names into IP addresses so that users do not need to remember the numerical addresses of websites they wish to access.

Basics of Cloud Computing

Cloud computing is a way of delivering computing services like storage, processing power, and software over the internet. Resources hosted on remote servers can be accessed rather than depending on local hardware alone.

Key Features of Cloud Computing:

On-demand Access:-Resources are available anytime, anywhere.

Scalability: - Users can increase or decrease resources according to their needs.

Cost-efficiency: - Eliminates the requirement of expensive hardware.

Types of Cloud Services: -

1. Infrastructure as a Service (IaaS): -

   Provides virtual machines, storage, and networks.

   Example: - Amazon Web Services (AWS).

2. Platform as a Service (PaaS): -

Offers platforms for the development of applications without the management of underlying infrastructure.

Example: - Google App Engine.

3. Software as a Service (SaaS): -

Provides software applications over the internet.

Example: - Microsoft Office 365.

Applications of Cloud Computing: -

Storing files on platforms like Google Drive or Dropbox.

Running applications without installing them locally.

Hosting websites and managing databases.

Networking is the heart of modern technology, and it makes possible easy communication and resource sharing. Starting from the type of networks to understanding the OSI model and then further to the concepts of IP addresses and cloud computing, networking basics form the backbone of digital connectivity. Mastering the basics is the only way forward for any person looking to navigate the digital world.

9. Storage and Database Management

In computing, storage, and database management are key components in organizing, storing, and retrieving data effectively. Whether it is saving your favorite pictures or managing vast amounts of business data, knowing how storage and databases work can help optimize performance and ensure data security.

Primary vs. Secondary Storage

Primary Storage (Volatile)

Primary storage, also called main memory, is where the computer stores data temporarily that is being used or processed. This memory is fast but volatile; this means that when the computer is turned off, all the data is lost.

Random Access Memory (RAM):-

RAM is the most common type of primary storage.

It holds data that is currently being accessed by the CPU, such as running programs or open files.

RAM is fast, meaning that it provides rapid access to data, thereby enhancing overall system performance.

Example: - Whenever you open an application, it loads into RAM so that the CPU can access it quickly.

Read-only Memory (ROM): -

ROM is used to store critical system information that doesn’t change, such as the computer's firmware (the BIOS or boot system).

It is non-volatile, which means it retains its data even when the computer is powered off.

Example: - The code that starts up the computer when you press the power button is stored in ROM.

Secondary Storage (Non-volatile)

Secondary storage refers to the devices that store data permanently. Unlike primary storage, secondary storage retains data even if the power is turned off, which makes it suitable for long-term data storage.

Hard Disk Drive (HDD): -

HDDs are magnetic storage devices that store large amounts of data.

They are relatively slow compared to other types of storage but offer larger capacities at a lower cost.

Example: - The majority of computers use HDDs to store the OS, applications, and user files.

Solid-state Drive (SSD): -

They are faster than HDDs since they store data on flash memory chips, not spinning disks.

More expensive but far faster and more durable, as they contain no moving parts.

Example: - Most of the modern laptops and gaming consoles use SSDs because they can load things very fast and boot up even faster.

Database Concepts

A database is a collection of structured data which can be accessed easily, managed, and updated. Databases are considered crucial in storing information in a manner that is both well-organized and efficient.

Tables, Records, and Fields

Tables: -

A database is made of one or more tables. Each table is used to store data in rows and columns, almost similar to a spreadsheet.

Example: A table named "Students" could hold details such as name, age, and grade for each student.

Records:

A record is a collection of related information in a table. It is a single entry in a table.

Each record is located in one row.

For instance- Information about a student might be represented by a single record in the "Students" table as follows- "John Doe, 15, 9th Grade."

Fields: -

Fields refer to individual data points contained within a record. They align to the columns in a table.

For instance- the "Students" table could include "Name," "Age," and "Grade."

Types of Databases

Databases come in different kinds, each having its purposes and suited to specific types of data and use cases.

1. Relational Databases

Relational databases apply tables, called relations, as the methods of storing the data. Each table in a relational database is related to others and is usually using a key field.

Structure: - Data in relational databases is arranged in rows and columns, and the relationship between the data is established using foreign keys.

Example: - Some of the most popular relational databases include MySQL, PostgreSQL, and Oracle Database.

Use Case: - Relational databases are most suitable for applications requiring complex querying and transactions, like banking systems or customer relationship management (CRM) systems.

2. NoSQL Databases

Definition: - NoSQL databases are designed for handling large volumes of unstructured or semi-structured data that don't fit well into tables.

Structure: - These databases use various structures, such as document stores, key-value pairs, graphs, or wide-column stores, instead of traditional rows and columns.

Example: - MongoDB, Cassandra, and Redis are well-known NoSQL databases.

Use Case: - NoSQL databases are widely used in big data applications, content management systems, and real-time web applications.

Storage and Data Backup Best Practices

Proper data storage and backup strategies are important for ensuring data security and integrity. Here are some best practices for managing storage and backing up data: -

1. Organize Your Data Efficiently

Use folders and subfolders to logically categorize your files. For instance, separate your documents from work files.

Label your files with meaningful names to avoid confusion and retrieve them easily.

2. Periodic Backups

Back up your data periodically. That way, if the worst happens - your hardware crashes, data is lost, or something else - you will not lose everything.

Practice using the 321-backup rule, as recommended. For example, one keeps 3 copies of your data, 2 formats among these which one stores separately, such as storing external drives and cloud storage of 1 copy off-site in the cloud platform.

3. Use Cloud Storage as a form of Redundancy

Cloud storage is very easy and secure to make backups of data. Many services provide cloud-based solutions for storing files, such as Google Drive, Dropbox, or OneDrive.

Cloud storage is also available remotely, allowing access from any device that has internet connectivity.

4. Store Several Copies of Backup Locations

In addition to using cloud storage, use an external drive or network-attached storage (NAS) to hold backups.

This ensures that you have different copies of your data at different physical locations, therefore reducing the risk of losing data.

5. Automatic Backups

Most cloud storage services and external hard drives allow you to automatically set up backups. With this, your data gets backed up regularly without you ever having to remember.

6. Regular Disk Cleanups

As time passes, useless files and temporary files pile up on your hard drives and other storage units, reducing their speed. Clean the disks at intervals to remove all old files.

7. Encrypt Your Data

Encrypting your files means that, even when lost or stolen, unauthorized persons cannot access your files.

Many cloud providers and devices allow built-in encryption.

8. Storage Health Monitoring

Regularly inspect the health of your hard drives and other storage. Most modern drives come with tools that can alert one about any failures so that you make backup copies before it may be too late.

Storage as well as database management are components of modern computing, particularly handling large volumes of data; and security and organization are necessary. The various types of storage devices, the basic concepts behind databases, and proper backup strategies all play a significant role in maintaining data integrity and optimizing your computer system's performance. Using the correct storage strategy and type of database to suit the requirements will ensure that you increase the efficiency and security levels of your data management systems.

10. Cybersecurity

In this age of the computer and internet, where the majority of people work, seek education, and carry out various personal activities, cybersecurity is more vital than ever. Cybersecurity refers to the protection of computers, networks, and data from any malicious attack, unauthorized access, and damage. Therefore, sensitive information must remain safe and ensure that the systems are operational without disturbance.

Importance of Cybersecurity in Today's World

With the increasing dependence on technology, cybersecurity is no longer an option but a necessity. Here are some reasons why cybersecurity is important: -

1. Protection of Personal Information: - Every day, people share personal details online, from email addresses and passwords to banking and medical information. Cybersecurity helps protect this data from being stolen or misused.

2. Avoiding Financial Loss: - Cyber-attacks can lead to serious financial losses, in terms of identity theft,

fraudulent transactions, or ransom payments. Cybersecurity is effective for the prevention of such loss.

3. Protection of Infrastructure: - Many crucial services, like hospitals, transport systems, and utility systems, rely on technology. A cyber-attack on such services could create chaos. Cybersecurity can be used for the protection of such infrastructure from cyber-attacks.

4. Maintaining Trust: - Whether for businesses or individuals, trust is vital. When systems are secure, customers and users feel confident sharing information and engaging online. Cybersecurity helps maintain this trust.

5. National Security: - Countries face cybersecurity threats from criminal organizations, terrorists, and even state-sponsored actors. Protecting government systems, military data, and critical infrastructure from cyber threats is vital for national security.

Common Cybersecurity Threats

While the internet makes life much easier, it brings along a lot of threats too. Therefore, it becomes very important to understand these threats so that people can take measures to defend themselves against them.

1. Viruses

Virus is a malicious program attached to some legitimate file or program. Once executed, it may spread to other systems, damage, or steal information. Viruses are transferred through email attachments, infected websites, or an external device like a USB drive.

2. Malware

Malware is an all-inclusive term, referring to any kind of malicious program intended to harm or take advantage of a computer system. Malware can come in the form of viruses, worms, Trojans, and spyware. Malware can steal sensitive information, damage files, and allow backdoors for attackers to operate the system remotely.

3. Phishing

It refers to tricking people to surrender secret information, such as the user name, passwords, or even their credit card details. Normally, the phishing attacks would usually entail fraudulent emails, sites, or messages that would pose like a legitimate service. They aim to lure in a victim to open malicious links or download corrupted files.

4. Ransomware

Ransomware is a kind of malware that locks or encrypts a victim's files and demands a ransom in exchange for restoring access. It can hit individuals, businesses, and even government institutions. Ransomware spreads through email attachments, malicious websites, or compromised software downloads.

Preventive Measures

Though cyber threats are changing with every passing day, there are still some preventive measures you can take to secure your data and devices.

1. Antivirus Software

Antivirus software is a program designed to detect, prevent, and remove viruses and other forms of malware from your computer. It scans files and programs for potential threats and alerts you if something suspicious is detected. Some popular antivirus software includes Norton, McAfee, and Bitdefender.

How it Helps: - Antivirus software continuously monitors your system for malicious activity and automatically updates to protect against new threats.

2. Firewalls

A firewall sits between your computer or network and the rest of the world, monitoring incoming and outgoing traffic and blocking potentially damaging information or unauthorized access attempts.

How it Helps: - Firewalls help in preventing unauthorized users from accessing your network while protecting your devices from outer threats. They can either be hardware-based (physical devices) or software-based (installed programs on your computer).

3. Secure Browsing

Secure browsing involves practices that help protect your personal information while browsing the internet. This includes using secure websites (those with "https" in the URL), avoiding clicking on suspicious links, and never sharing sensitive information on unsecured websites.

How it Helps: - Secure browsing will minimize the risk of falling victim to phishing attacks, malware infections, and other online threats. In addition, tools such as browser extensions that block popups or track cookies can further enhance your security.

4. Strong Passwords and Multifactor Authentication (MFA)

A password should be tough to guess for others; it is a combination of the upper and lowercase letters, numbers, and symbols. Multifactor authentication increases security because more than one form of verification is needed, such as a password and a verification code that is sent to your phone.

How it Helps: - It helps protect your online accounts from unauthorized access by cybercriminals, making it harder for them to steal your information.

Introduction to Ethical Hacking

Ethical hacking, also referred to as Whitehat hacking, is the process of checking computer systems, networks, or applications for vulnerabilities that could be exploited by malicious hackers. Ethical hackers use the same tools and techniques as cybercriminals but with the goal of improving security rather than exploiting it.

Role of Ethical Hackers

Penetration Testing: -Ethical hackers perform penetration testing, which is referred to as pen testing, identifying weaknesses in a system through which an attacker can make an entry. It ensures that vulnerabilities are addressed before they are exploited.

Security Audits: -They carry out security audits, evaluating the overall security of a system and provide improvements for the same.

Incident Response: - Ethical hackers aid organizations in responding to cyber threats by investigating breaches and strategizing on ways to avoid future attacks.

How Ethical Hacking Works

Ethical hackers work on the consent of the organization to test their systems. They use the same techniques as malicious hackers, but their actions are authorized and aimed at improving security.

The findings from the ethical hacking activities are used to strengthen the security measures and ensure protection of sensitive data and systems from cyber threats.

With the increased amount of technology being integrated into our daily lives, cybersecurity has never been more essential. Viruses and malware to phishing and ransomware are some of the cyber threats that can be quite devastating to individuals and organizations alike. We can protect ourselves and our data by understanding these threats and implementing preventive measures such as antivirus software, firewalls, and secure browsing habits. Moreover, ethical hacking plays a key role in the proactive identification and fixing of vulnerabilities, so our systems remain secure in an ever-evolving digital world.

11. Programming Basics

Programming is a basic skill that lets people communicate with computers and make them perform specific tasks. It means writing a set of instructions in a programming language the computer can understand and execute. Programming is a process through which people design software, apps, websites, games, etc. If one has no background in programming, this sounds like rocket science. Break it down, though, and you get an easy to understand it. In this section, we'll explore the basics of programming, programming languages, how to write your first program, and how to execute and debug it.

What is Programming?

Programming, also known as coding or software development, is the process of writing instructions for computers to follow. These instructions, called programs, tell the computer how to perform specific tasks, such as performing calculations, processing data, or displaying information.

Computers are very efficient at performing jobs, but they do not understand the human language. That's where programming comes in. By using programming languages, we can bridge the gap between humans and machines. A program, therefore, is a collection of instructions telling the computer exactly how to carry out something.

That's almost like giving the computer a recipe to follow. Like how you follow a recipe to make a dish, the computer follows instructions in the program to execute an action.

Overview of Programming Languages

A programming language is a language used to write programs. It provides the rules for constructing instructions that a computer can execute. There are many programming languages, each suited for different tasks, but most programming languages share common principles.

Some of the most popular programming languages include: -

1. Python

What it is: - Python is a high-level, easy-to-read programming language that is mostly suggested for beginners. It's widely used in web development, data analysis, AI, and automation.

Why it's good for beginners: - The syntax of Python is quite simple, meaning it is easier to write and understand. Thus, it's one of the best choices for someone who is just beginning to learn programming.

Common applications: - For developing websites, data analytics, automation of tasks, and development of machine learning models.

2. Java

What is it: Java is an object-oriented general-purpose programming language that is used to create large-scale applications. Its main applications are in the fields of Android app development and enterprise software.

Why it's important: - Java does not depend on a particular platform because it can run anywhere where there is a virtual machine of Java installed.

Common applications: - android apps, web applications, backend services, and games.

3. C++

What is it: - C++ is a powerful, high-performance programming language widely applied in systems programming and game development. It gives finer control over hardware and system resources.

Why is it significant: - C++ finds its applications in places that require performance and efficiency- game engines and operating systems.

Common applications: - Game development, operating systems, desktop applications, and high-performance computing.

While these languages differ in syntax and purpose, they all help you solve problems and produce applications.

Writing Your First Program

Writing your first program can be exhilarating, and it's much simpler than you may have initially thought. Let's look at Python for an example, as it's also one of the more forgiving languages.

Here is how to write a simple program that prints a message to the screen:

Explanation: - This program uses the `print()` function to print the text "Hello, world!" on the screen.

What happens: - When you run the program, the computer will follow the instructions inside the parentheses and show the message on your screen.

Steps to write and run this program: -

1. Open a code editor or an online Python compiler (e.g., Replit or IDLE).

2. Type the code `print("Hello, world!")`.

3. Run the program by clicking the "Run" button or typing the command in the terminal.

4. The output will appear on the screen, showing "Hello, world!"

Congratulations! You've written and run your first program.

Program Execution

Once you've written your program, it's time to execute (or run) it. Execution refers to the process of the computer following the instructions you've written in the program. Here's a step-by-step breakdown of the execution process: -

1. Writing the Code: - First, you write your code using a programming language (e.g., Python, Java, C++).

2. Compilation/Interpretation: The code will be compiled or interpreted depending on your language. Compiling is when before executing the code gets converted into the

machine language so the computer will understand. Interpreted language: where the program compiles it into machine code as and when it's going to be executed.

Python is an interpreted language so doesn't need a compilation before running.

Java is compiled into bytecode, which is then interpreted by the Java Virtual Machine (JVM).

C++ is compiled into machine code before execution.

3. Running the Program: - Once compiled or interpreted, the program is executed, and the computer follows the instructions to produce the desired output, such as printing text or doing calculations.

Debugging is the process of finding and fixing errors or bugs in your program. Bugs are mistakes or issues that cause a program to behave unexpectedly. Debugging is an essential skill for every programmer because it helps ensure that your program works correctly.

Common Types of Bugs

Syntax errors: - These occur when the code does not follow the rules of the programming language (e.g., missing parentheses, misspelled keywords).

Runtime errors: - These occur when the program is running, for example, dividing by zero or accessing invalid data.

Logic errors: - These are errors in the program's logic, where the program runs but does not output the correct result.

How to Debug a Program

1. Read the error messages: - Most programming languages give error messages that can help you find out where the problem is.

2. Carefully check your code: - Go over your code and look for errors in missing punctuation, wrong variables, or misspelled words.

3. Print statements: - Place print statements throughout your code to output variable values or the state of the program. This will help pinpoint where things are going wrong.

4. Utilize debugging tools: Most code editors or integrated development environments (IDEs) include built-in debugging tools. These allow you to step through your program, see variable values, and diagnose bugs much more easily.

Programming is the basis of the modern digital world, allowing people to create everything from simple websites and apps to intricate software systems. Learning programming basics, such as an understanding of programming languages such as Python, Java, and C++, and writing simple programs as well as learning how to debug them, can unlock so many possibilities.

12. Microsoft Office

Microsoft Office is one of the most widely used productivity software suites in the world. It contains powerful tools that help people create documents, analyze data, and deliver presentations. Whether you are a student, a professional, or just someone looking to organize personal projects, MS Office has something to offer. In this section, we will explore the key applications of Microsoft Office: - MS Word, MS Excel, and MS PowerPoint. We'll also discover some advanced tips and tricks to help you work more efficiently.

MS Word: - Creating and Formatting Documents

MS Word is a word processing software that enables you to create, edit, and format text documents. This is one of the most commonly used tools for writing reports, essays, letters, and even books. Let's look at some of the basic features and functions of MS Word.

Creating a New Document

1. Open MS Word, and click on "Blank Document" or choose from a template.

2. Type your text. MS Word automatically adjusts text size and spacing.

Formatting Text

1. Font Style and Size: You can change the font style, size, and color from the options provided in the toolbar. The most used fonts are Arial, Times New Roman, and Calibri.

2. Bold, Italic, and Underline: Select the text and click on the bold (B), italic (I), or underline (U) button to emphasize your words.

3. Paragraph Formatting: - Change alignment (left, center, right, justify) and line spacing. You can also use bullet points or numbered lists for better organization.

Headings and Subheadings

1. Use Heading 1, Heading 2, and other heading styles for better structure.

2. Headings help readers scan the document and find the relevant section.

Inserting Images and Tables

1. Click on Insert, then Pictures to insert pictures from your computer or online sources.

2. For tables, click on Insert Table, choose the number of rows and columns, and fill in the data.

Saving and Sharing Documents

1. Save your document regularly using Ctrl + S or by clicking on the Save button.

2. MS Word saves your file either in the format of.docx,.pdf or .txt.

MS Excel: - Basic Formulas, Charts, and Data Analysis

MS Excel is another type of spreadsheet application through which one can organize analyze data and visualize it on screen. It is applied widely in budgeting and financial analysis and is even used to manage projects.

Formulas in Excel

Formulas are what provide the backbone for Excel; that is, they do everything to perform calculations based on addition, subtraction, multiplication, and division, such as: -

SUM: - Adds a row of numbers. For instance, `=SUM (A1: -A5)`

AVERAGE: - Calculates the average number based on a range. Example: - `=AVERAGE (B1: -B5)`

IF: - It does conditional logic, whereby: - `=IF(C1>10, "Pass", "Fail")`

COUNT: - Counts the number of cells that contain numbers. Example: - `=COUNT(D1: -D10)`

Charts and Graphs

Excel enables you to create different types of charts to visualize your data. This can help in understanding trends, comparisons, and distributions.

1. Select your data: - Highlight the data range you want to visualize.

2. Add a Chart: Click the Insert tab, then select the chart type best describing your data. It may be any kind of bar, line, or pie chart.

3. Format the Chart: You will also have the option of changing the colors, the title, and the axis title so the chart may become more understandable, yet very aesthetic.

Tools for Data Analysis

1. Filters: - You can apply filters to sort and reorganize data according to certain criteria. For example, you can filter all sales above a certain number.

2. Pivot Tables: - You can sum up large amounts of data with pivot tables. Data can be easily organized and analyzed by categories such as date, product type, or region.

3. Conditional Formatting: Highlight cells that meet specific criteria, such as values greater than 1000, to make your data analysis more visual.

MS PowerPoint: - Presentations

MS PowerPoint is used to create interesting presentations. It's perfect for school projects, business meetings, and conferences. Whether you are presenting a sales report or a research project, PowerPoint helps you display information clearly and professionally.

Creating a New Slide

1. Open MS PowerPoint and start with a blank presentation or select a template.

2. To add a new slide, click Home > New Slide. You can choose from different layouts, including Title Slide, Title and Content, Comparison, and more.

Adding Text, Images, and Graphics

1. Text: - Click in the text boxes to add text to any slide. You can change the font, size, and color as you would in MS Word.

2. Images: - Click on Insert > Pictures to insert pictures from your computer or the web.

3. Shapes and Icons: - Add shapes, arrows, and icons from the Insert tab to give your slides a design facelift.

Transitions and Animations

1. Slide Transitions: You can add transitions to your slides so that they come in with different effects such as fade, wipe, or zoom.

2. Animations: You can add animations to text and objects on your slides. For example, you can make text appear one line at a time or objects move across the screen.

Presenting the Slideshow

To begin presenting the slideshow, click Slide Show > From Beginning or press F5.

2. Navigation: During the presentation, you can navigate between slides using the arrow keys or mouse clicks.

Advanced Tips and Tricks for MS Office

Now that we have covered the basics, let's dive into some advanced tips and tricks that can make your MS Office experience more efficient and productive.

1. Keyboard Shortcuts

Using keyboard shortcuts can save you a lot of time. Some useful shortcuts include:

Ctrl + C:

Copy

Ctrl + V: - Paste

Ctrl + X: - Cut

Ctrl + Z: - Undo

Ctrl + Y: - Redo

Ctrl + S: - Save

2. Templates

MS Office has multiple predesigned templates for documents, spreadsheets, and presentations. Use this template to create a very professional-looking document quickly. To access templates, select File > New, and search for a template that suits your needs.

3. Collaboration

Features

MS Office will enable you to share the same document with your fellow individuals in real-time especially for online versions of Office, (Office 365)

Share Documents: You are allowed to share Word, Excel, or PowerPoint files, thus other individuals can view or even edit the document at a particular time.

Comments and Track Changes: - You can leave a note or feedback about documents using comments. Track changes enable you to see changes others have made.

4. MS Office in the Cloud

Cloud integration lets you store your MS Office files in OneDrive, Google Drive, or Dropbox so that you access your documents from anywhere in the world and share them with others.

5. Automating Tasks with Macros (Excel and Word)

A macro is a sequence of commands and instructions that can be triggered to automate repetitive tasks. For instance, you can record a macro to format a document or generate reports in Excel.

Microsoft Office is a powerful suite of applications that can help you perform a variety of tasks efficiently, from creating documents to analyzing data and delivering presentations. Mastering the basics of MS Word, Excel, and PowerPoint, and utilizing advanced tips and tricks, can make you more productive and organized in your daily tasks.

13. Flowcharts and problem-solving

What is a Flowchart?

A flowchart is a pictorial presentation of any process or workflow. It depicts various symbols joined through arrows representing steps in sequence. Flowcharts are typically used for problem-solving, programming, and process designing. It is helpful in the breakdown of complex tasks into simpler manageable components and shows exactly how one step leads to another.

Symbols and Their Meanings

The use of symbols to depict an action or a decision varies according to type within a flowchart. Common types include -

Oval: It describes starting or finishing the process

Rectangle: Describes some kind of process or actions

Diamond: Represents an on-decision point with two flows as conditions decide for a different action.

Parallelogram: Describing input and output where some data might be entering a system, and the others will result from processing and should be outputted.

Arrow: - Demonstrates the direction of the flow and shows how the symbols are joined.

How to Design Flowcharts for Solving Logical problems

In developing an effective flowchart, here are the steps one can follow: -

1. Identify the Problem: - Understand the task or problem to be solved.

2. Define the Steps: - The process is divided into logical steps. Each will have a symbol representing that particular step.

3. Symbols: Use the correct symbols at each step of the process, decision, input, and output.

4. Connect Symbols: Use arrows to represent the flow of one step to another.

5. Review and Test: Check if the flowchart is reasonable and solves the problem in a logical sequence. It should be intelligible and understandable.

Flowcharts can be beneficial in programming by using them to outline algorithms or find practical applications to real-world problems, and then applied in industries like engineering, business, or even healthcare sectors.

Computer Shortcut Keys and Abbreviations

Important Shortcut Keys to Efficiency

The computer shortcut keys allow one to accomplish any task quickly, completing the activity with only some key combination. The most basic shortcuts include:

Ctrl + C: Copy selected item(s).

Ctrl + V: Paste the copied item(s).

Ctrl + X- Cut the selected item(s)

Ctrl + Z- Undo the last action

Ctrl + Y- redo the last undone action.

Ctrl + A- to select all items on current screen or document.

Ctrl + S- Save the present document or file.

Alt + Tab- to switch the open applications.

Ctrl + P- to print out the present document or screen.

Ctrl + F: - Open the Find function to search within a document or webpage.

These shortcuts will save time for you and make your work much more efficient. Editing a document, browsing through the web, or just managing files would be less laborious if done with keyboard shortcuts instead of using the mouse to accomplish a task.

Commonly Used Abbreviations in Computing

Computing is replete with technical terms, and many of these terms are abbreviated for convenience. Here are some of the most common abbreviations: -

CPU: - Central Processing Unit — The brain of the computer, responsible for executing instructions.

RAM: - Random Access Memory — A type of computer memory that stores data for active programs.

ROM: - Read-only Memory — Non-volatile memory used for firmware and system booting.

URL: - Uniform Resource Locator — The address of a resource on the web, also referred to as a website address.

IP: - Internet Protocol — A set of rules for sending data over networks.

DNS: - Domain Name System — The system that translates domain names into IP addresses.

HTTP: - Hypertext Transfer Protocol — The protocol used to transfer web pages over the internet.

HTML: - Hypertext Markup Language — The language used to design and format web pages.

USB: - Universal Serial Bus — A set of standards for attaching peripheral devices to a computer.

These abbreviations are part of computer jargon. Knowing them facilitates your understanding of technical vocabulary and enhances your performance working in a computer-based context.

Computer Viruses Viruses and Cyber Threats What Are Computer Viruses?

A computer virus is a form of malware that replicates itself and can spread from one computer to another. Viruses often attach themselves to files or programs, and when the infected file is opened, the virus activates, potentially damaging the system or stealing data.

Viruses can cause a number of problems, including:

Slowing down the computer's performance

Deleting files or corrupting data

Stealing personal information or passwords

Compromising system security

Types of Malware and How They Spread

Malware is a broad term for any malicious software, including viruses, worms, trojans, and ransomware. Here are some common types: -

Viruses: - As mentioned earlier, viruses attach to files and spread when the infected file is opened.

Worms: - Worms are self-replicating programs that can spread over networks without any user action.

Trojans: - Trojans masquerade as legitimate software but cause harm when executed.

Ransomware: - This kind of malware blocks users from accessing their files and then demands a ransom to open them again.

The virus can be spread in several ways: downloading an infected file, clicking on a malicious email link, or using infected USB drives.

Methods to Eradicate and Prevent Virus Infections

To guard your computer from viruses and malware:

1. Install Antivirus Software: - Use antivirus programs capable of detecting and removing dangers.

2. Keep Updated: - Keep your os, software, and virus software updated to protect newer threats.

3. Avert Suspicious Links: - Do not click suspicious links or download attachments when receiving them from unknown contacts.

4. Use the Firewall: - Activate firewall systems in your computer networks.

5. Backup Your Files: - Regularly back up important files to protect against ransomware attacks.

6. Scan Regularly: - Run regular virus scans to detect any hidden malware.

Through these steps, you are able to minimize the risk of viruses and other malware impacting your computer.

Websites and Web Browsers

What is a Website?

A website refers to a collection of interlinked web pages that are made available on the internet. Websites can be used to present information, sell a product, or offer some other service. They are housed on web servers and accessible from a web browser by simply typing the website's URL.

Components of a Website

A website is comprised of several components that coordinate to present content:

HTML (Hypertext Markup Language): - A programming code that is considered a basis for structuring a website's content.

CSS (Cascading Style Sheets): - CSS defines styles and layouts for HTML content, controlling features like color, font, and space.

JavaScript: - The programming language that adds interactive components to a website. That can be form validations, animations, and more sophisticated content updates.

Those building blocks are used in concert to create userfriendly interactive websites.

Popular Web Browsers and Their Features

Web browsers are programs used to access websites. The most popular browsers include: -

Google Chrome: - Known for speed and performance, with a vast selection of extensions.

Mozilla Firefox: - Offers privacy features and customizability.

Microsoft Edge: - The default browser on Windows, built for speed and security.

Safari: - Apple's browser, optimized for macOS and iOS devices.

Every browser has its unique features, but they all enable a user to browse the internet, access websites, and manage bookmarks.

Safe Browsing Tips

To be safe while browsing the web:

1. Use Strong Passwords: - Do not use easy to guess passwords for your accounts.

2. Look for HTTPS: - Ensure that the website uses HTTPS (not HTTP), which secures your data.

3. Do not click on suspicious links: Click on pop-ups or links in emails with caution.

4. Update your browser: Update your browser from time to time to resolve security vulnerabilities.

5. Install security extensions: Make use of ad blockers and privacy protectors, among other extensions that will secure your browser.

Through the safe browsing habits, you will be safe from all the online threats.

Advanced Topics in Computer Management

Virtual Memory Allocation

Virtual memory is a technique of memory management where a computer can compensate for physical memory shortages by temporarily transferring data from RAM to disk storage. This makes the computer believe that it has more memory than it does, so it can run more programs simultaneously.

Disk Access and File Systems

The purpose of the file system is that of storing and accessing data from the disk. It therefore maintains files in directories. They also assign metadata on this file to locate. For a file system, two well-known ones are: NTFS (Windows) and HFS (Mac). This is disk access - The way the operating system goes about reading and writing the data to the devices.

Interrupt and Time Sharing Management

Interrupt handling is the process of dealing with events that need the computer's immediate attention, such as hardware failures or user inputs. Timesharing systems allow multiple users or tasks to share the computer's resources efficiently by dividing time into small intervals.

Security in System Design

System security is critical to safeguard data and prevent unauthorized users from accessing the system. The measures that come in place for security include encryption, authentication, firewalls, and access control policies. Security best practices protect against breaches and guard sensitive information.

We have explored several important topics related to computers in this book. Starting from the basics of hardware and software to more advanced topics such as cybersecurity and networking, these concepts are highly crucial in today's technology-driven world.

Emerging Technologies: - AI, IoT, Blockchain

The computing future is very exciting with so many emerging technologies. AI is changing the world as it enables machines to learn and make decisions. The Internet of Things connects objects to the Internet, creating a smarter world. Blockchain offers secure, decentralized transactions that can revolutionize industries like finance and healthcare.

The world of computing is ever-evolving. To stay ahead of the curve, it's essential to keep learning and exploring new technologies. For a beginner or an experienced user, there is always something new to discover. Just keep experimenting, stay curious, and embrace the future of technology.

Practice MCQ s

1. What is a computer?

a) A manual tool for solving problems

b) An electronic device that processes data

c) A machine for storing liquids

d) A mechanical transportation device

Answer: - b) An electronic device that processes data

2. What code do computers operate on?

a) Hexadecimal code

b) Binary code

c) Octal code

d) Decimal code

Answer: - b) Binary code

3. Binary code is made up of: -

a) Letters AZ

b) 0s and 1s

c) Images and symbols

d) All of the above

Answer: - b) 0s and 1s

4. Which is NOT a characteristic of a computer?

a) Precision

b) Versatility

c) Instantaneous processing

d) Unlimited memory capacity

Answer: - d) Unlimited memory capacity

5. Computers are primarily used for: -

a) Manual calculations

b) Executing instructions and solving problems

c) Producing physical objects

d) Writing books automatically

Answer: - b) Executing instructions and solving problems

History of Computers

6. The abacus was invented around: -

a) 2400 BCE

b) 1600 BCE

c) 1940 CE

d) 400 BCE

Answer: - a) 2400 BCE

7. Blaise Pascal developed which device?

a) Analytical Engine

b) ENIAC

c) Pascaline

d) Abacus

Answer: - c) Pascaline

8. Charles Babbage is known as: -

a) The inventor of ENIAC

b) The father of the computer

c) A pioneer of modern AI

d) A scientist in quantum mechanics

Answer: - b) The father of the computer

9. What was the purpose of the Difference Engine?

a) Generalpurpose computation

b) Arithmetic problem solving

c) Data storage

d) Realtime simulations

Answer: - b) Arithmetic problem solving

10. The first programmable digital computer was: -

a) Zuse Z3

b) ENIAC

c) UNIVAC

d) IBM PC

Answer: - a) Zuse Z3

11. ENIAC was built in: -

a) 1941

b) 1945

c) 1939

d) 1952

Answer: - b) 1945

12. The second generation of computers introduced: -

a) Transistors

b) Vacuum tubes

c) Integrated Circuits (ICs)

d) Artificial intelligence

Answer: - a) Transistors

13. Integrated Circuits were introduced in: -

a) The first generation

b) The second generation

c) The third generation

d) The fifth generation

Answer: - c) The third generation

14. Personal computers became common during which generation?

a) Second generation

b) Fourth generation

c) Fifth generation

d) Third generation

Answer: - b) Fourth generation

15. Quantum computing is associated with: -

a) First generation

b) Second generation

c) Fifth generation

d) Fourth generation

Answer: - c) Fifth generation

16. Computers in education provide: -

a) Chalkboards and textbooks

b) Access to vast resources and elearning tools

c) Instant physical libraries

d) None of the above

Answer: - b) Access to vast resources and elearning tools

17. In healthcare, computers are used for: -

a) Diagnosing diseases

b) Performing robotic surgeries

c) Managing patient records

d) All of the above

Answer: - d) All of the above

18. Telemedicine allows for: -

a) Online gaming

b) Remote healthcare services

c) Video conferencing for education

d) Conducting scientific experiments

Answer: - b) Remote healthcare services

19. Which of these is an example of communication technology enabled by computers?

a) Letter writing

b) Emails and video calls

c) Telephone booths

d) Satellite launches

Answer: - b) Emails and video calls

20. Ecommerce platforms rely on computers for: -

a) Online shopping

b) Offline banking

c) Designing physical stores

d) Managing transportation systems

Answer: - a) Online shopping

21. In science, computers are used for: -

a) Simulating physical phenomena

b) Data analysis

c) Genetic research

d) All of the above

Answer: - d) All of the above

22. What role do computers play in entertainment?

a) Broadcasting radio signals

b) Gaming, video editing, and streaming

c) Conducting live sports

d) Printing newspapers

Answer: - b) Gaming, video editing, and streaming

23. What technology powers selfdriving vehicles?

a) Steam engines

b) Computer algorithms and AI

c) Electromagnetic waves

d) Manual programming

Answer: - b) Computer algorithms and AI

24. Computers in government services help: -

a) Manage taxes

b) Deliver public services digitally

c) Conduct elections

d) All of the above

Answer: - d) All of the above

25. Computers are used in traffic management to: -

a) Control signals and monitor flow

b) Print traffic tickets

c) Repair roads

d) Communicate via radio

Answer: - a) Control signals and monitor flow

26. Which tool is considered the precursor to modern computing?

a) Abacus

b) ENIAC

c) UNIVAC

d) Difference Engine

Answer: - a) Abacus

27. How do computers transform transportation?

a) By providing GPS navigation

b) Designing vehicles

c) Enabling autonomous cars

d) All of the above

Answer: - d) All of the above

28. Computers in education enable: -

a) Virtual classrooms

b) Instant communication with teachers

c) Elearning tools and simulations

d) All of the above

Answer: - d) All of the above

29. Artificial intelligence in fifthgeneration computers helps with: -

a) Gaming

b) Image recognition

c) Natural language processing

d) All of the above

Answer: - d) All of the above

30. Which industry heavily relies on computers for simulations and virtual testing?

a) Agriculture

b) Manufacturing

c) Construction

d) Fashion

Answer: - b) Manufacturing

31. Computers in scientific research help: -

a) Conduct largescale data analysis

b) Simulate natural phenomena

c) Explore space missions

d) All of the above

Answer: - d) All of the above

32. What is the primary use of GPS technology powered by computers?

a) Traffic reporting

b) Navigation and route planning

c) Vehicle repairs

d) Entertainment in vehicles

Answer: - b) Navigation and route planning

33. Elearning platforms like Coursera and Khan Academy rely on computers for: -

a) Offline workshops

b) Online course delivery and interactive tools

c) Printing educational materials

d) Teacher recruitment

Answer: - b) Online course delivery and interactive tools

34. Telemedicine is an example of how computers are transforming: -

a) Education

b) Banking

c) Healthcare

d) Agriculture

Answer: - c) Healthcare

35. Which of the following technologies enables virtual reality (VR) applications?

a) Steam engines

b) Computer algorithms and simulations

c) Satellite transmission

d) Manual animations

Answer: - b) Computer algorithms and simulations

36. The Analytical Engine was designed to: -

a) Perform addition only

b) Introduce programmability to computing

c) Store physical records

d) Control electricity flow

Answer: - b) Introduce programmability to computing

37. The first generation of computers was based on which technology?

a) Transistors

b) Integrated circuits

c) Vacuum tubes

d) Microprocessors

Answer: - c) Vacuum tubes

38. Which invention replaced vacuum tubes in the second generation of computers?

a) Microprocessors

b) Transistors

c) Diodes

d) Motherboards

Answer: - b) Transistors

39. Which generation of computers saw the introduction of integrated circuits?

a) First generation

b) Second generation

c) Third generation

d) Fourth generation

Answer: - c) Third generation

40. Personal computers became widely available during which era?

a) First generation

b) Fourth generation

c) Second generation

d) Fifth generation

Answer: - b) Fourth generation

41. Computers in agriculture help: -

a) Monitor soil health

b) Automate irrigation systems

c) Predict weather patterns

d) All of the above

Answer: - d) All of the above

42. Roboticassisted surgeries are possible because of: -

a) Cloud storage

b) Highperformance computing and AI

c) Mechanical engineering alone

d) Satellite technology

Answer: - b) Highperformance computing and AI

43. Cloud storage is primarily used for: -

a) Temporary backups only

b) Accessing data from remote servers online

c) Archiving paper records

d) Compressing large files offline

Answer: - b) Accessing data from remote servers online

44. What role do computers play in the entertainment industry?

a) Editing videos

b) Powering gaming consoles

c) Streaming online content

d) All of the above

Answer: - d) All of the above

45. In transportation, autonomous vehicles rely on: -

a) Manual controls

b) Preprogrammed algorithms and sensors

c) Satellite phone networks

d) Mechanical levers

Answer: - b) Preprogrammed algorithms and sensors

46. Binary code represents data using: -

a) 0s and 1s

b) Letters and numbers

c) Pictures and symbols

d) All of the above

Answer: - a) 0s and 1s

47. What does the CPU primarily do in a computer?

a) Store data permanently

b) Execute instructions and process data

c) Display visual content

d) None of the above

Answer: - b) Execute instructions and process data

48. Which part of the computer is known as its "brain"?

a) GPU

b) CPU

c) RAM

d) ROM

Answer: - b) CPU

49. Artificial intelligence primarily uses: -

a) Quantum mechanics

b) Machine learning algorithms

c) Solar energy

d) Satellite technology

Answer: - b) Machine learning algorithms

50. Quantum computing is associated with: -

a) Fifthgeneration computers

b) Firstgeneration computers

c) Cloud computing

d) None of the above

Answer: - a) Fifthgeneration computers

51. What is the primary function of a computer?

a) Manual data processing

b) Electronic data processing

c) Performing only arithmetic calculations

d) Only storing data

Answer: - b) Electronic data processing

52. What is binary code made up of?

a) Letters and symbols

b) 0s and 1s

c) Numbers and special characters

d) None of the above

Answer: - b) 0s and 1s

53. Which device is considered the first general purpose electronic computer?

a) Zuse Z3

b) ENIAC

c) UNIVAC

d) Analytical Engine

Answer: - b) ENIAC

54. The fifth generation of computers focuses on: -

a) Vacuum tubes

b) Transistors

c) Artificial intelligence

d) Integrated circuits

Answer: - c) Artificial intelligence

55. Which of these is not a field transformed by computers?

a) Education

b) Healthcare

c) Communication

d) None of the above

Answer: - d) None of the above

56. What is software?

a) Tangible computer parts

b) Programs and instructions for a computer

c) Physical storage devices

d) Hardware components

Answer: - b) Programs and instructions for a computer

57. Which of the following is an input device?

a) Monitor

b) Printer

c) Keyboard

d) Speaker

Answer: - c) Keyboard

58. What does RAM stand for?

a) Random Access Memory

b) ReadOnly Memory

c) Read Access Memory

d) None of the above

Answer: - a) Random Access Memory

59. Which hardware component is considered the "brain" of the computer?

a) Hard disk

b) CPU

c) Monitor

d) GPU

Answer: - b) CPU

60. What does an operating system do?

a) Executes user applications

b) Manages hardware resources

c) Provides a user interface

d) All of the above

Answer: - d) All of the above

61. Computers primarily operate using which number system?

a) Decimal

b) Binary

c) Octal

d) Hexadecimal

Answer: - b) Binary

62. Which logic gate produces an output of 1 when both inputs are 1?

a) AND gate

b) OR gate

c) NOT gate

d) XOR gate

Answer: - a) AND gate

63. The NOT gate: -

a) Inverts the input signal

b) Adds two inputs

c) Outputs 1 if both inputs are 1

d) None of the above

Answer: - a) Inverts the input signal

64. How many possible states are there in binary?

a) 10

b) 2

c) 8

d) 16

Answer: - b) 2

65. Hexadecimal numbers are based on: -

a) Base 8

b) Base 16

c) Base 10

d) Base 2

Answer: - b) Base 16

66. What is the primary purpose of computer networking?

a) Isolating data

b) Sharing resources and information

c) Increasing computer size

d) Deleting data

Answer: - b) Sharing resources and information

67. Which device is used to connect different networks?

a) Router

b) Monitor

c) Keyboard

d) RAM

Answer: - a) Router

68. What does IP stand for in networking?

a) Internet Protocol

b) Internal Process

c) Integrated Program

d) Information Packet

Answer: - a) Internet Protocol

69. Which type of network covers a small geographic area like a home or office?

a) WAN

b) LAN

c) MAN

d) PAN

Answer: - b) LAN

70. The full form of WiFi is: -

a) Wireless Fidelity

b) Wide Frequency

c) Wireless Framework

d) None of the above

Answer: - a) Wireless Fidelity

71. Cloud computing allows users to: -

a) Store data on remote servers

b) Build physical servers

c) Use computers without a power source

d) None of the above

Answer: - a) Store data on remote servers

72. What is the primary goal of cybersecurity?

a) Deleting unnecessary files

b) Protecting systems from unauthorized access

c) Formatting hard drives

d) Increasing CPU speed

Answer: - b) Protecting systems from unauthorized access

73. Artificial intelligence refers to: -

a) A type of CPU

b) Machines that simulate human intelligence

c) Highspeed internet

d) A computer brand

Answer: - b) Machines that simulate human intelligence

74. Which of the following is an example of cloud storage?

a) Google Drive

b) Microsoft Word

c) Hard Disk Drive

d) RAM

Answer: - a) Google Drive

75. What technology is used for virtual reality (VR)?

a) Cloud computing

b) GPUs and specialized headsets

c) Data compression algorithms

d) Email software

Answer: - b) GPUs and specialized headsets

Basic Computer Components: - Hardware and Software

1. What is hardware?

a) Programs and data

b) Physical components of a computer

c) Software utilities

d) None of the above

Answer: - b) Physical components of a computer

2. Which of the following is an example of an input device?

a) Monitor

b) Printer

c) Keyboard

d) Speaker

Answer: - c) Keyboard

3. Which hardware component is considered the "brain" of the computer?

a) Hard disk

b) CPU

c) Motherboard

d) RAM

Answer: - b) CPU

4. What is the primary function of RAM?

a) Permanent data storage

b) Temporary data storage for quick access

c) Displaying graphics

d) Managing input and output devices

Answer: - b) Temporary data storage for quick access

5. What does the motherboard do?

a) Powers the computer

b) Connects all hardware components

c) Processes instructions

d) Stores data

Answer: - b) Connects all hardware components

6. Which of the following is an output device?

a) Mouse

b) Printer

c) Keyboard

d) Scanner

Answer: - b) Printer

7. What is the role of the Power Supply Unit (PSU)?

a) Execute programs

b) Convert electricity for computer components

c) Store data

d) Manage input devices

Answer: - b) Convert electricity for computer components

8. What is software?

a) Tangible computer parts

b) Programs and instructions for a computer

c) Physical storage devices

d) None of the above

Answer: - b) Programs and instructions for a computer

9. Which software category includes operating systems?

a) System software

b) Application software

c) Utility software

d) Networking software

Answer: - a) System software

10. What is an example of utility software?

a) Microsoft Word

b) Antivirus software

c) Google Chrome

d) Adobe Photoshop

Answer: - b) Antivirus software

11. What is the smallest unit of data in a computer?

a) Byte

b) Bit

c) Word

d) Character

Answer: - b) Bit

12. How many bits are there in a byte?

a) 4

b) 8

c) 16

d) 32

Answer: - b) 8

13. Which of the following is an example of an operating system?

a) Google Chrome

b) Windows 10

c) Microsoft Office

d) Zoom

Answer: - b) Windows 10

14. What is a file?

a) A collection of physical documents

b) A storage device

c) A collection of digital data

d) A program

Answer: - c) A collection of digital data

15. What does a firewall do?

a) Prevents unauthorized access to a network

b) Converts data into binary

c) Improves system performance

d) Manages storage devices

Answer: - a) Prevents unauthorized access to a network

16. What is the first step in the Input Processing Output cycle?

a) Output

b) Processing

c) Storage

d) Input

Answer: - d) Input

17. Which device is used for processing data in a computer?

a) RAM

b) CPU

c) Monitor

d) USB drive

Answer: - b) CPU

18. What does the fetch decode execute cycle refer to?

a) Data storage process

b) Program execution process

c) File management system

d) Antivirus operation

Answer: - b) Program execution process

19. In networking, what are data packets?

a) Physical storage units

b) Segments of data sent over a network

c) Devices for storing data

d) Programs for analyzing data

Answer: - b) Segments of data sent over a network

20. Which protocol ensures data reaches its destination accurately?

a) RAM

b) TCP/IP

c) GPU

d) HTML

Answer: - b) TCP/IP

21. What does HDD stand for?

a) High Density Drive

b) Hard Disk Drive

c) Heavy Duty Device

d) Hard Data Drive

Answer: - b) Hard Disk Drive

22. Which is faster: - SSD or HDD?

a) SSD

b) HDD

c) Both are equal

d) Depends on the system

Answer: - a) SSD

23. What type of memory is volatile?

a) RAM

b) ROM

c) HDD

d) SSD

Answer: - a) RAM

24. What does USB stand for?

a) Universal Storage Backup

b) Unified System Bus

c) Universal Serial Bus

d) Unlimited System Backup

Answer: - c) Universal Serial Bus

25. What is primary storage?

a) RAM

b) SSD

c) HDD

d) USB

Answer: - a) RAM

26. What is cloud computing?

a) Computing in remote locations

b) Storing and accessing data over the internet

c) Using highspeed processors

d) Building private networks

Answer: - b) Storing and accessing data over the internet

27. What does AI stand for?

a) Advanced Internet

b) Artificial Intelligence

c) Automated Integration

d) Applied Information

Answer: - b) Artificial Intelligence

28. Which is an example of cloud storage?

a) RAM

b) Google Drive

c) SSD

d) USB drive

Answer: - b) Google Drive

29. What is a common cybersecurity threat?

a) SSD

b) Firewall

c) Virus

d) RAM

Answer: - c) Virus

30. What does encryption do?

a) Stores data

b) Protects data by converting it into code

c) Deletes unnecessary files

d) Optimizes computer speed

Answer: - b) Protects data by converting it into code

31. What is an example of an application software?

a) Operating system

b) Google Chrome

c) Motherboard

d) Power Supply Unit

Answer: - b) Google Chrome

32. Which device connects computers in a network?

a) Router

b) Printer

c) Monitor

d) RAM

Answer: - a) Router

33. What is the full form of WiFi?

a) Wide Frequency

b) Wireless Fidelity

c) Wireless Framework

d) None of the above

Answer: - b) Wireless Fidelity

34. What type of software is Linux?

a) Application software
b) System software
c) Utility software
d) Firmware
Answer: - b) System software

35. What is the purpose of an antivirus program?

a) Enhance performance
b) Prevent unauthorized access
c) Detect and remove malicious software
d) Backup files
Answer: - c) Detect and remove malicious software

36. What is an example of secondary storage?

a) RAM
b) HDD
c) CPU
d) GPU
Answer: - b) HDD

37. Which of the following is a biometric security method?

a) Password
b) Fingerprint scanner
c) Firewall
d) Encryption
Answer: - b) Fingerprint scanner

38. What is a computer virus?
a) A physical component
b) Malicious software designed to harm systems
c) An outdated operating system
d) A program that speeds up computers
Answer: - b) Malicious software designed to harm systems

39. What is the primary function of a GPU?
a) Data storage
b) Process graphics and videos
c) Manage memory
d) Execute code
Answer: - b) Process graphics and videos

40. What does TCP/IP stand for?
a) Transmission Control Protocol/Internet Protocol
b) Total Communication Protocol/Internal Protocol
c) Transfer Control Program/Input Program
d) Transmitted Connection Protocol/Internet Path
Answer: - a) Transmission Control Protocol/Internet Protocol

41. Which of the following is not an input device?
a) Scanner
b) Microphone
c) Monitor

d) Webcam
Answer: - c) Monitor

42. What type of device is a touch screen?
a) Input device
b) Output device
c) Both input and output device
d) Neither input nor output
Answer: - c) Both input and output device

43. Which device outputs hard copies of documents?
a) Monitor
b) Printer
c) USB drive
d) Scanner
Answer: - b) Printer

44. What is the main function of a speaker?
a) Display visual data
b) Input sound data
c) Output audio data
d) Process sound data
Answer: - c) Output audio data

45. Which of the following devices captures images or videos?
a) Printer

b) Webcam
c) Microphone
d) Monitor
Answer: - b) Webcam

46. What is the main purpose of networking?
a) Data storage
b) Sharing data and resources
c) Running antivirus scans
d) Increasing processing speed
Answer: - b) Sharing data and resources

47. What does LAN stand for?
a) Local Area Network
b) Large Access Node
c) Linked Area Network
d) Local Application Network
Answer: - a) Local Area Network

48. What is the internet?
a) A type of CPU
b) A global network of interconnected computers
c) A utility software
d) A type of memory
Answer: - b) A global network of interconnected computers

49. What is the primary function of a router?
a) Store data
b) Connect devices to a network
c) Process data
d) Protect against viruses
Answer: - b) Connect devices to a network

50. What does IP in IP address stand for?
a) Internal Process
b) Internet Protocol
c) Input Program
d) Intelligent Path
Answer: - b) Internet Protocol

51. Which of the following is NOT a cybersecurity threat?
a) Virus
b) Malware
c) Firewall
d) Phishing
Answer: - c) Firewall

52. What is phishing?
a) A type of virus
b) Fraudulent attempts to obtain sensitive information
c) Data backup technique
d) Computer optimization process
Answer: - b) Fraudulent attempts to obtain sensitive information

53. What is encryption used for?
a) Creating files
b) Securing data by converting it into unreadable code
c) Deleting unnecessary data
d) Optimizing computer speed
Answer: - b) Securing data by converting it into unreadable code

54. What is the purpose of a firewall?
a) Securely delete files
b) Manage internal storage
c) Monitor and control network traffic
d) Execute programs
Answer: - c) Monitor and control network traffic

55. What does HTTPS signify in a URL?
a) A faster network connection
b) Secure communication over the internet
c) A type of virus
d) A standard file type
Answer: - b) Secure communication over the internet

56. What is artificial intelligence?
a) The physical design of computers
b) The simulation of human intelligence by machines
c) A type of storage device
d) A networking protocol

Answer: - b) The simulation of human intelligence by machines

57. Which technology allows data to be stored and accessed remotely?
a) Cloud computing
b) Networking
c) RAM
d) SSD
Answer: - a) Cloud computing

58. What is a smart device?
a) A high performance computer
b) An electronic device that connects to a network for enhanced functionality
c) A backup tool for data
d) A type of processor
Answer: - b) An electronic device that connects to a network for enhanced functionality

59. What is virtual reality (VR)?
a) A data storage method
b) A simulated digital environment
c) A networking protocol
d) An operating system
Answer: - b) A simulated digital environment

60. Which is an example of AI-powered software?

a) Microsoft Word
b) ChatGPT
c) Windows 10
d) Antivirus
Answer: - b) ChatGPT

66. What component processes instructions and data in a computer?

a) CPU

b) GPU

c) RAM

d) Hard drive

Answer: - a) CPU

67. What is the purpose of a GPU?

a) Store data

b) Render images and videos

c) Execute basic instructions

d) Connect peripherals

Answer: - b) Render images and videos

68. Which hardware component connects all other components in a computer?

a) Hard drive

b) Motherboard

c) RAM

d) Power supply

Answer: - b) Motherboard

69. What is the role of the power supply unit (PSU)?

a) Store energy

b) Process data

c) Convert electricity for computer use

d) Generate images

Answer: - c) Convert electricity for computer use

70. What is an example of a hybrid device that acts as both input and output?

a) Scanner

b) Touchscreen

c) Monitor

d) Printer

Answer: - b) Touchscreen

71. Which type of memory is volatile?

a) SSD

b) RAM

c) ROM

d) HDD

Answer: - b) RAM

72. What is the main characteristic of primary storage?

a) Long term storage

b) Portable

c) Fast but temporary

d) Slow but permanent

Answer: - c) Fast but temporary

73. Which of these is not an example of secondary storage?

a) Hard disk drive

b) RAM

c) Solid-state drive

d) USB flash drive

Answer: - b) RAM

74. What type of storage is typically used for cloud computing?

a) Local hard drive

b) Optical disc

c) Remote servers

d) USB drive

Answer: - c) Remote servers

75. Which device is used for optical storage?

a) SSD

b) HDD

c) DVD

d) RAM

Answer: - c) DVD

76. Which term describes storage on a network that multiple devices can access?

a) Cloud storage

b) RAM

c) Local storage

d) Cache

Answer: - a) Cloud storage

77. Which type of storage has no moving parts?

a) Hard drive

b) DVD

c) Solid-state drive

d) CDROM

Answer: - c) Solid-state drive

78. What does RAID stand for in storage systems?

a) Random Access Integrated Devices

b) Redundant Array of Independent Disks

c) Rapid Access Input Devices

d) Remote Automated Interactive Disks

Answer: - b) Redundant Array of Independent Disks

79. What unit is used to measure storage capacity?

a) GHz

b) Pixels

c) Bytes

d) DPI

Answer: - c) Bytes

80. What is the primary purpose of cache memory?

a) Long term storage

b) Improve data transfer speeds

c) Generate images

d) Connect peripherals

Answer: - b) Improve data transfer speeds

81. Which of the following is an example of system software?

a) Microsoft Word

b) Google Chrome

c) Windows 10

d) VLC Media Player

Answer: - c) Windows 10

82. What is the function of an operating system?

a) Process data

b) Manage hardware and software

c) Store files

d) Perform backups

Answer: - b) Manage hardware and software

83. Which type of software is used for creating presentations?

a) Spreadsheet software

b) Word processor

c) Presentation software

d) Web browser

Answer: - c) Presentation software

84. What is an example of utility software?

a) Disk cleanup

b) Photoshop

c) Browser

d) Calculator

Answer: - a) Disk cleanup

85. What is a kernel in an operating system?

a) Hardware component

b) Core part of the OS managing resources

c) A type of application software

d) Antivirus software

Answer: - b) Core part of the OS managing resources

86. Which of the following is opensource software?

a) macOS

b) Linux

c) Microsoft Office

d) Adobe Photoshop

Answer: - b) Linux

87. What does GUI stand for?

a) General User Interface

b) Graphical User Interface

c) Global User Interface

d) Graphics Utility Integration

Answer: - b) Graphical User Interface

88. What is an application suite?

a) A single app

b) A collection of related applications

c) A programming tool

d) An antivirus software

Answer: - b) A collection of related applications

89. Which type of software allows users to browse the internet?

a) Media player

b) Spreadsheet software

c) Web browser

d) Database management software

Answer: - c) Web browser

90. What is the main difference between proprietary and opensource software?

a) Opensource software is always free, and proprietary is not.

b) Opensource allows modification, while proprietary does not.

c) Proprietary software is safer.

d) Proprietary software is faster.

Answer: - b) Opensource allows modification, while proprietary does not.

91. What does AI stand for?

a) Automatic Intelligence

b) Artificial Intelligence

c) Automated Integration

d) Advanced Internet

Answer: - b) Artificial Intelligence

92. What is cloud computing?

a) Running programs on the local hard drive

b) Storing data and accessing services over the internet

c) Using computers in outer space

d) A type of antivirus software

Answer: - b) Storing data and accessing services over the internet

93. What is an example of IoT (Internet of Things)?

a) A traditional desktop computer

b) A smart thermostat

c) A USB flash drive

d) An external monitor

Answer: - b) A smart thermostat

94. Which field studies quantum computers?

a) Cryptography

b) Quantum computing

c) Mechanical engineering

d) Electrical installation

Answer: - b) Quantum computing

95. What is the main benefit of blockchain technology?

a) It generates data faster.

b) It provides a decentralized ledger system.

c) It improves hardware efficiency.

d) It creates secure hardware devices.

Answer: - b) It provides a decentralized ledger system.

96. What does VR stand for?

a) Virtual Reality

b) Variable Response

c) Verified Resources

d) Visual Recording

Answer: - a) Virtual Reality

97. Which technology uses AI to simulate human conversations?

a) Chatbots

b) Firewalls

c) Blockchain

d) SSDs

Answer: - a) Chatbots

98. What is an essential characteristic of 5G networks?

a) Increased energy consumption

b) Highspeed connectivity

c) Low network capacity

d) Reduced global coverage

Answer: - b) Highspeed connectivity

99. What is the primary purpose of machine learning?

a) To process data storage

b) To enable computers to learn from data

c) To replace hardware components

d) To build internet browsers

Answer: - b) To enable computers to learn from data

100. Which technology powers virtual assistants like Siri and Alexa?

a) Networking

b) Artificial Intelligence

c) Quantum computing

d) Cloud storage

Answer: - b) Artificial Intelligence

Computer Hardware MCQs

1. What is computer hardware?

a) The intangible part of the computer

b) The physical and tangible part of the computer system

c) Software components

d) None of the above

Answer: - b) The physical and tangible part of the computer system

2. Which of the following is an input device?

a) Monitor

b) Printer

c) Mouse

d) Speaker

Answer: - c) Mouse

3. Which type of keyboard is most commonly used?

a) Mechanical

b) Ergonomic

c) QWERTY

d) Wireless

Answer: - c) QWERTY

4. What is the function of a scanner in a computer system?

a) To display information

b) To convert physical documents into digital format

c) To store data

d) To process graphics

Answer: - b) To convert physical documents into digital format

5. Which of the following is an output device?

a) Microphone

b) Printer

c) Keyboard

d) Mouse

Answer: - b) Printer

6. Which device is used to produce audio output?

a) Monitor

b) Printer

c) Speakers

d) Scanner

Answer: - c) Speakers

7. What type of storage device is a hard disk drive (HDD)?

a) Primary storage

b) Optical storage

c) Secondary storage

d) Flash storage

Answer: - c) Secondary storage

8. Which of the following is faster than a Hard Disk Drive (HDD)?

a) SSD (SolidState Drive)

b) USB Drive

c) Optical Discs

d) Flash Drive

Answer: - a) SSD (Solid State Drive)

9. Which of the following is an example of an optical storage device?

a) SSD

b) USB Drive

c) CD

d) RAM

Answer: - c) CD

10. What does RAM stand for?

a) ReadAccess Memory

b) Random Access Memory

c) Ready Access Memory

d) Remote Access Memory

Answer: - b) Random Access Memory

11. What is the role of a CPU in a computer?

a) To manage all hardware components

b) To process instructions and perform calculations

c) To store data

d) To display information

Answer: - b) To process instructions and perform calculations

12. What does the Control Unit (CU) in the CPU do?

a) Performs arithmetic and logical operations

b) Manages memory access

c) Directs the flow of data and instructions within the computer

d) Handles graphic processing

Answer: - c) Directs the flow of data and instructions within the computer

13. What is the function of the Arithmetic Logic Unit (ALU)?

a) It stores data temporarily

b) It performs mathematical and logical operations

c) It directs the flow of instructions

d) It displays graphical information

Answer: - b) It performs mathematical and logical operations

14. Which of the following is a specialized processor used for rendering graphics?

a) CPU

b) RAM

c) GPU

d) Hard Drive

Answer: - c) GPU

15. Which component connects all hardware components together in a computer?

a) CPU

b) GPU

c) Motherboard

d) RAM

Answer: - c) Motherboard

16. What is the function of a cooling system in a computer?

a) To store data

b) To manage the computer's memory

c) To prevent overheating of components

d) To enhance graphic performance

Answer: - c) To prevent overheating of components

17. Which of the following is a type of secondary storage?

a) CPU

b) RAM

c) Hard Drive

d) Register

Answer: - c) Hard Drive

18. How do input devices communicate with the computer?

a) By transferring data through the motherboard

b) By converting data into digital form

c) By sending electrical signals to the storage devices

d) By displaying data directly

Answer: - b) By converting data into digital form

19. What is the primary function of an operating system?

a) To manage hardware resources

b) To run applications

c) To handle internet connectivity

d) To display content

Answer: - a) To manage hardware resources

20. Which operating system is known for its userfriendly interface and wide compatibility?

a) macOS

b) Linux

c) Windows

d) Ubuntu

Answer: - c) Windows

21. Which of the following is an example of utility software?

a) Word Processor

b) Antivirus Software

c) Web Browser

d) Database Management

Answer: - b) Antivirus Software

22. What is the role of drivers in a computer system?

a) To display content on the screen

b) To manage memory usage

c) To enable communication between the operating system and hardware devices

d) To enhance the visual output

Answer: - c) To enable communication between the operating system and hardware devices

23. Which of the following is an example of application software?

a) Windows OS

b) File Explorer

c) Microsoft Word

d) Device Manager

Answer: - c) Microsoft Word

24. What is the purpose of a web browser?

a) To create documents

b) To browse the internet

c) To manage hardware resources

d) To edit images

Answer: - b) To browse the internet

25. What does the acronym “USB” stand for?

a) Universal Serial Bus

b) United System Bus

c) Universal Service Bus

d) Unified Storage Bus

Answer: - a) Universal Serial Bus

26. What is the function of an operating system?

a) To provide a platform for running applications

b) To process data

c) To store user files

d) To capture video and audio

Answer: - a) To provide a platform for running applications

27. Which of the following is not a productivity software?

a) Microsoft Excel

b) Google Docs

c) Adobe Photoshop

d) Microsoft PowerPoint

Answer: - c) Adobe Photoshop

28. What is the function of the motherboard in a computer?

a) To process data

b) To connect and allow communication between components

c) To store data permanently

d) To handle input and output

Answer: - b) To connect and allow communication between components

29. Which of the following is a primary storage device?

a) SSD

b) USB Drive

c) Hard Drive

d) Optical Disc

Answer: - a) SSD

30. What type of memory is volatile and gets wiped when the computer is turned off?

a) ROM

b) Flash Memory

c) RAM

d) Hard Drive

Answer: - c) RAM

31. What is the main difference between primary and secondary storage?

a) Primary storage is slower than secondary storage

b) Secondary storage is temporary, while primary storage is permanent

c) Primary storage is faster and volatile, while secondary storage is slower and non-volatile

d) Secondary storage has more capacity than primary storage

Answer: - c) Primary storage is faster and volatile, while secondary storage is slower and non-volatile

32. What type of storage device is a Solid State Drive (SSD)?

a) Primary storage

b) Secondary storage

c) Optical storage

d) Volatile memory

Answer: - b) Secondary storage

33. Which of the following is a common use for a scanner?

a) To play audio files

b) To convert physical documents into digital format

c) To process graphical images

d) To store data

Answer: - b) To convert physical documents into digital format

34. What is the main purpose of a graphics processing unit (GPU)?

a) To manage data storage

b) To execute logic operations

c) To render graphics, videos, and animations

d) To control the power supply

Answer: - c) To render graphics, videos, and animations

35. Which device converts digital signals into sound?

a) Printer

b) Microphone

c) Speakers

d) Monitor

Answer: - c) Speakers

36. What does BIOS stand for in relation to a computer's motherboard?

a) Basic Integrated Operating System

b) Basic Input Output System

c) Binary Input Operating System

d) Binary Integrated Operating System

Answer: - b) Basic Input Output System

37. Which of the following is not a type of RAM?

a) DRAM

b) SRAM

c) ESDRAM

d) SSD

Answer: - d) SSD

38. Which type of software enables communication between the operating system and external hardware?

a) Utility Software

b) Drivers

c) Application Software

d) Security Software

Answer: - b) Drivers

39. Which of the following is a utility software?

a) Microsoft Word

b) Disk Cleanup Tool

c) Google Chrome

d) Adobe Photoshop

Answer: - b) Disk Cleanup Tool

40. What is the function of an antivirus software?

a) To monitor memory usage

b) To provide internet access

c) To protect against malware and viruses

d) To help store data

Answer: - c) To protect against malware and viruses

41. Which software is used to organize and store data in a tabular form?

a) Spreadsheet software

b) Word processing software

c) Web browser

d) Media player

Answer: - a) Spreadsheet software

42. What is the most common operating system used in smartphones?

a) Linux

b) iOS

c) Windows

d) Android

Answer: - b) iOS

43. Which of the following is a feature of macOS?

a) Developed by Google

b) Known for its security and performance

c) Used primarily for gaming

d) Free and opensource

Answer: - b) Known for its security and performance

44. Which software is typically used for creating presentations?

a) Microsoft Excel

b) Microsoft Word

c) Microsoft PowerPoint

d) Microsoft Access

Answer: - c) Microsoft PowerPoint

45. What is the key difference between opensource and proprietary software?

a) Opensource software is free, while proprietary software is paid

b) Opensource software has a user friendly interface, while proprietary software does not

c) Opensource software is only for personal use, while proprietary software can be used commercially

d) Opensource software is owned by a company, while proprietary software is not

Answer: - a) Opensource software is free, while proprietary software is paid

46. Which of the following is an example of opensource software?

a) Microsoft Office

b) Adobe Photoshop

c) LibreOffice

d) Final Cut Pro

Answer: - c) LibreOffice

47. What is an example of proprietary software?

a) Google Chrome

b) Firefox

c) Microsoft Windows

d) Linux

Answer: - c) Microsoft Windows

48. Which of the following is not a feature of Linux?

a) Opensource

b) Free to use

c) Proprietary

d) Customizable

Answer: - c) Proprietary

49. What does the term "cloud storage" refer to?

a) Storage located within a computer’s internal hard drive

b) The temporary storage of data during processing

c) Storage of data on remote servers accessible via the internet

d) Storage devices connected via USB

Answer: - c) Storage of data on remote servers accessible via the internet

50. Which of the following is an example of a cloud storage provider?

a) USB Drive

b) Google Drive

c) Hard Disk Drive

d) SSD

Answer: - b) Google Drive

51. Which type of device is commonly used for video conferencing?

a) Scanner

b) Webcam

c) Printer

d) Speaker

Answer: - b) Webcam

52. What is the purpose of a motherboard in a computer system?

a) To control all software applications

b) To connect the CPU, memory, and other components together

c) To manage power supply

d) To store data

Answer: - b) To connect the CPU, memory, and other components together

53. Which of the following is not an example of application software?

a) Adobe Photoshop

b) Google Chrome

c) Windows 10

d) Microsoft Excel

Answer: - c) Windows 10

54. What does the acronym "OS" stand for?

a) Open Source

b) Operating Software

c) Operating System

d) Online System

Answer: - c) Operating System

55. What is the role of system software?

a) To help run specific applications

b) To manage the computer's hardware and provide a platform for running applications

c) To display graphics

d) To manage the internet connection

Answer: - b) To manage the computer's hardware and provide a platform for running applications

56. Which of the following software types is used for specific tasks like word processing or creating spreadsheets?

a) Utility Software

b) Application Software

c) System Software

d) Network Software

Answer: - b) Application Software

57. Which of the following is an opensource web browser?

a) Google Chrome

b) Mozilla Firefox

c) Microsoft Edge

d) Safari

Answer: - b) Mozilla Firefox

58. What does RAM store in a computer system?

a) Data that is not currently being processed

b) Temporary data that is actively used by the processor

c) Software applications

d) Permanent storage of documents

Answer: - b) Temporary data that is actively used by the processor

59. Which of the following is not considered an input device?

a) Microphone

b) Printer

c) Scanner

d) Camera

Answer: - b) Printer

60. What is an example of a utility software tool?

a) Google Chrome

b) Disk Cleanup

c) Microsoft PowerPoint

d) Skype

Answer: - b) Disk Cleanup

61. Which of the following is a characteristic of secondary storage?

a) It is faster than primary storage

b) It is non-volatile, meaning data is retained when the power is off

c) It is used for temporary storage during processing

d) It requires frequent updates

Answer: - b) It is non-volatile, meaning data is retained when the power is off

62. What is the primary function of the CPU (Central Processing Unit)?

a) To store data permanently

b) To execute instructions and perform calculations

c) To manage peripheral devices

d) To display visual output

Answer: - b) To execute instructions and perform calculations

63. What type of device is an optical disk (CD, DVD, Bluray)?

a) Primary storage

b) Secondary storage

c) Input device

d) Output device

Answer: - b) Secondary storage

64. Which of the following is an example of a volatile memory?

a) Hard Disk

b) USB Drive

c) RAM

d) ROM

Answer: - c) RAM

65. What does the Control Unit (CU) of the CPU do?

a) Performs logical operations

b) Directs the flow of data and instructions within the computer

c) Manages the storage devices

d) Provides communication with external devices

Answer: - b) Directs the flow of data and instructions within the computer

66. Which of the following is a type of input device?

a) Printer

b) Monitor

c) Keyboard

d) Speaker

Answer: - c) Keyboard

67. Which component is most responsible for generating graphics in video games?

a) CPU

b) GPU

c) RAM

d) Hard Drive

Answer: - b) GPU

68. Which of the following storage devices is known for its fast read/write speeds?

a) Hard Disk Drive (HDD)

b) Solid State Drive (SSD)

c) CD

d) Bluray Disk

Answer: - b) Solid State Drive (SSD)

69. What is the main function of the motherboard in a computer?

a) To store data

b) To provide cooling to the CPU

c) To allow communication between the CPU, RAM, and other components

d) To display output to the user

Answer: - c) To allow communication between the CPU, RAM, and other components

70. What is the main function of the ALU (Arithmetic Logic Unit) in the CPU?

a) It performs calculations and logical operations

b) It controls data flow between devices

c) It stores instructions

d) It manages the power supply

Answer: - a) It performs calculations and logical operations

71. Which of the following is an example of output software?

a) Google Chrome

b) Microsoft Excel

c) Adobe Acrobat Reader

d) Microsoft Word

Answer: - c) Adobe Acrobat Reader

72. Which of the following is an example of a utility software?

a) Adobe Photoshop

b) Disk Cleanup

c) Microsoft Word

d) Mozilla Firefox

Answer: - b) Disk Cleanup

73. What does "cloud storage" allow users to do?

a) Store data on local hard drives

b) Store data remotely on servers accessible via the internet

c) Increase RAM capacity

d) Back up files to optical media

Answer: - b) Store data remotely on servers accessible via the internet

74. Which of the following is NOT an example of an output device?

a) Printer

b) Headphones

c) Scanner

d) Monitor

Answer: - c) Scanner

75. What is the main function of drivers in a computer system?

a) To increase processing speed

b) To enable the operating system to communicate with hardware

c) To prevent malware attacks

d) To store data on secondary storage

Answer: - b) To enable the operating system to communicate with hardware

76. What is the key feature of opensource software?

a) It is available for purchase

b) It is free to use and the source code is publicly available

c) It requires a subscription for access

d) It cannot be modified or shared

Answer: - b) It is free to use and the source code is publicly available

77. Which of the following is an example of proprietary software?

a) LibreOffice

b) GIMP

c) Microsoft Office

d) VLC Media Player

Answer: - c) Microsoft Office

78. What does "ROM" stand for in a computer system?

a) Read-only Memory

b) Random Only Memory

c) Real Operational Memory

d) Rotational Output Memory

Answer: - a) Read-only Memory

79. What type of device is a webcam?

a) Input device

b) Output device

c) Storage device

d) Processing device

Answer: - a) Input device

80. What is the main benefit of using cloud storage over traditional hard drives?

a) Faster processing speed

b) Larger storage capacity

c) Access to files from anywhere via the internet

d) Lower risk of data loss

Answer: - c) Access to files from anywhere via the internet

81. Which of the following is a type of non-volatile memory?

a) RAM

b) Cache memory

c) ROM

d) Registers

Answer: - c) ROM

82. Which of the following operating systems is opensource?

a) Windows

b) macOS

c) Linux

d) iOS

Answer: - c) Linux

83. What is the function of a power supply in a computer?

a) To store data

b) To convert electrical energy into usable power for the components

c) To cool down the components

d) To manage memory allocation

Answer: - b) To convert electrical energy into usable power for the components

84. Which of the following is a common feature of modern GPUs?

a) Used only for video games

b) Helps process parallel tasks in computing

c) Limited to rendering only 2D images

d) Cannot be upgraded or replaced

Answer: - b) Helps process parallel tasks in computing

85. What type of software would you use to browse the internet?

a) Media software

b) Web browser

c) Word processing software

d) Utility software

Answer: - b) Web browser

86. Which of the following storage devices is typically used to transfer data between computers?

a) Hard Disk Drive (HDD)

b) Solid State Drive (SSD)

c) USB Flash Drive

d) Optical Disc

Answer: - c) USB Flash Drive

87. What type of computer hardware is responsible for converting digital data to visual output?

a) CPU

b) RAM

c) Monitor

d) Hard Disk

Answer: - c) Monitor

88. What is the purpose of a fan in a computer system?

a) To process data

b) To provide network connectivity

c) To cool down components like the CPU and GPU

d) To store data

Answer: - c) To cool down components like the CPU and GPU

89. Which of the following is an example of cloud storage?

a) External hard drive

b) Google Drive

c) Optical disc

d) USB flash drive

Answer: - b) Google Drive

90. Which device would you use to capture audio input on a computer?

a) Microphone

b) Webcam

c) Keyboard

d) Monitor

Answer: - a) Microphone

91. Which of the following devices is used to store large amounts of data for long term use?

a) RAM

b) USB Drive

c) Solid State Drive (SSD)

d) Printer

Answer: - c) Solid State Drive (SSD)

92. Which type of storage is the fastest in terms of data access speed?

a) Hard Disk Drive (HDD)

b) RAM

c) Optical Disk

d) Solid State Drive (SSD)

Answer: - b) RAM

93. What does the motherboard in a computer primarily connect?

a) CPU, RAM, and hard drive

b) Input devices and output devices

c) Cooling systems and power supply

d) Web browsers and productivity software

Answer: - a) CPU, RAM, and hard drive

94. What is the main role of a graphics card (GPU) in a computer?

a) To perform mathematical operations

b) To process and render images and video

c) To manage data storage

d) To monitor the health of the system

Answer: - b) To process and render images and video

95. What is the most common use of a touchscreen in modern devices?

a) To input audio data

b) To control the device through physical buttons

c) To interact directly with the visual interface

d) To store information

Answer: - c) To interact directly with the visual interface

96. Which of the following is true about Random Access Memory (RAM)?

a) It is non-volatile

b) It stores data permanently

c) It is faster than secondary storage

d) It is used to store data even when the computer is off

Answer: - c) It is faster than secondary storage

97. Which of the following is a benefit of using an SSD over an HDD?

a) SSDs are slower than HDDs

b) SSDs are less durable

c) SSDs consume more power

d) SSDs have faster read and write speeds

Answer: - d) SSDs have faster read and write speeds

98. Which of the following is an example of an input device?

a) Monitor

b) Printer

c) Keyboard

d) Speaker

Answer: - c) Keyboard

99. Which type of operating system is macOS?

a) Opensource

b) Proprietary

c) Freeware

d) Cloud based

Answer: - b) Proprietary

100. Which of the following operating systems is free to use and opensource?

a) Windows

b) macOS

c) Linux

d) iOS

Answer: - c) Linux

101. What is the purpose of the BIOS in a computer?

a) To store files and documents

b) To manage system resources and start the computer

c) To process data

d) To control power management

Answer: - b) To manage system resources and start the computer

102. What does the term "volatility" refer to in memory?

a) The speed at which data is processed

b) The ability of memory to retain data when the power is off

c) The type of device that reads and writes data

d) The ease with which data is corrupted

Answer: - b) The ability of memory to retain data when the power is off

103. Which of the following is a feature of proprietary software?

a) Free to use

b) Source code is open and modifiable

c) Requires a license for use

d) Developed and maintained by the community

Answer: - c) Requires a license for use

104. Which device would you use to convert digital data into printed output?

a) Printer

b) Scanner

c) Monitor

d) Speaker

Answer: - a) Printer

105. What is the role of an operating system?

a) To store files

b) To run applications

c) To connect devices to the internet

d) To manage hardware resources and provide a user interface

Answer: - d) To manage hardware resources and provide a user interface

106. Which type of software is used for video conferencing?

a) Word Processor

b) Web Browser

c) Communication Software

d) Antivirus Software

Answer: - c) Communication Software

107. Which of the following is true about cloud storage?

a) It is not secure for storing sensitive data

b) It requires local storage devices for backup

c) It can be accessed from anywhere with an internet connection

d) It is limited to only storing photos and videos

Answer: - c) It can be accessed from anywhere with an internet connection

108. What is the primary function of the Arithmetic Logic Unit (ALU)?

a) To execute instructions

b) To perform mathematical and logical operations

c) To store data temporarily

d) To manage memory

Answer: - b) To perform mathematical and logical operations

109. Which of the following is an example of utility software?

a) Google Chrome

b) Windows Defender

c) VLC Media Player

d) Microsoft Excel

Answer: - b) Windows Defender

110. Which of the following storage devices is most commonly used for backup and portability?

a) Hard Disk Drive (HDD)

b) Solid State Drive (SSD)

c) USB Flash Drive

d) Optical Disc

Answer: - c) USB Flash Drive

111. Which type of memory is used to store the firmware of a computer?

a) RAM

b) ROM

c) Cache

d) Hard Drive

Answer: - b) ROM

112. Which of the following is the fastest form of memory?

a) Hard Disk

b) RAM

c) Cache

d) Optical Disk

Answer: - c) Cache

113. What does the operating system do during the bootup process?

a) Loads the firmware into memory

b) Processes user data

c) Initializes and tests hardware components

d) Displays the graphical user interface

Answer: - c) Initializes and tests hardware components

114. Which of the following is an example of system software?

a) Microsoft Word

b) Google Chrome

c) Linux

d) Adobe Photoshop

Answer: - c) Linux

115. What type of software is used to create spreadsheets?

a) Word Processor

b) Spreadsheet Software

c) Communication Software

d) Media Player

Answer: - b) Spreadsheet Software

116. What does "file management" software allow users to do?

a) Access the internet

b) Organize, copy, and delete files

c) Encrypt sensitive data

d) Perform mathematical operations

Answer: - b) Organize, copy, and delete files

117. Which of the following is an example of opensource software?

a) Microsoft Windows

b) Adobe Photoshop

c) LibreOffice

d) iTunes

Answer: - c) LibreOffice

118. What is the main difference between opensource and proprietary software?

a) Opensource software is free, while proprietary software must be purchased

b) Opensource software has limited functionality

c) Proprietary software is easier to use than opensource software

d) Opensource software is always less secure than proprietary software

Answer: - a) Opensource software is free, while proprietary software must be purchased

119. What is an example of a solid state storage device?

a) DVD

b) Flash Drive

c) Hard Disk Drive

d) Magnetic Tape

Answer: - b) Flash Drive

120. Which type of device is used to play back audio from a computer?

a) Printer

b) Microphone

c) Speakers

d) Camera

Answer: - c) Speakers

121. Which component is responsible for executing instructions in a computer system?

a) CPU

b) RAM

c) Motherboard

d) GPU

Answer: - a) CPU

122. What is the main function of a cooling system in a computer?

a) To store data

b) To manage power supply

c) To prevent components from overheating

d) To clean the components

Answer: - c) To prevent components from overheating

123. Which of the following is an example of output software?

a) Adobe Photoshop

b) Google Chrome

c) Microsoft PowerPoint

d) Operating System

Answer: - c) Microsoft PowerPoint

124. What is the purpose of a driver in a computer system?

a) To store files and applications

b) To enable communication between hardware and software

c) To execute mathematical calculations

d) To manage power consumption

Answer: - b) To enable communication between hardware and software

125. Which of the following is an example of an input device?

a) Monitor

b) Keyboard

c) Printer

d) Projector

Answer: - b) Keyboard

126. What does RAM stand for in computing?

a) Read and Modify

b) Random Access Memory

c) Rapid Active Memory

d) Readable Auxiliary Memory

Answer: - b) Random Access Memory

127. Which of the following is an example of secondary storage?

a) RAM

b) Hard Disk Drive (HDD)

c) CPU

d) Cache

Answer: - b) Hard Disk Drive (HDD)

128. What type of software is used to protect a computer from malware and viruses?

a) Antivirus Software

b) Word Processor

c) Web Browser

d) Spreadsheet Software

Answer: - a) Antivirus Software

129. What is the main difference between RAM and ROM?

a) RAM is volatile, while ROM is non-volatile

b) RAM stores long term data, while ROM stores temporary data

c) RAM is only used during bootup, while ROM is used during normal operations

d) RAM is slower than ROM

Answer: - a) RAM is volatile, while ROM is non-volatile

130. Which type of device is primarily used for pointing and clicking on graphical elements in a computer interface?

a) Keyboard

b) Printer

c) Mouse

d) Scanner

Answer: - c) Mouse

131. Which of the following is an example of system software?

a) Microsoft Word

b) Linux

c) Google Chrome

d) VLC Media Player

Answer: - b) Linux

132. Which of the following is the main advantage of using solid state drives (SSDs) over hard disk drives (HDDs)?

a) SSDs are less expensive

b) SSDs are faster and more durable

c) SSDs use magnetic storage

d) SSDs store data permanently

Answer: - b) SSDs are faster and more durable

133. What is the function of the motherboard in a computer?

a) To provide power to the CPU

b) To connect and integrate all the components of the computer

c) To store data permanently

d) To process graphical images

Answer: - b) To connect and integrate all the components of the computer

134. What type of memory is used for quick access to data frequently used by the CPU?

a) ROM

b) Cache

c) Flash Drive

d) Optical Disk

Answer: - b) Cache

135. What is the primary function of the CPU in a computer?

a) To manage storage devices

b) To display visual output

c) To perform calculations and execute instructions

d) To communicate with external devices

Answer: - c) To perform calculations and execute instructions

136. What is a common use for a scanner in a computer system?

a) To print documents

b) To display images on a screen

c) To convert physical documents into digital form

d) To store data

Answer: - c) To convert physical documents into digital form

137. Which of the following storage devices uses spinning disks to store data?

a) Solid State Drive (SSD)

b) Flash Drive

c) Optical Disc

d) Hard Disk Drive (HDD)

Answer: - d) Hard Disk Drive (HDD)

138. What is the role of an operating system in a computer?

a) To provide security

b) To control and manage hardware resources

c) To store user data

d) To connect the computer to the internet

Answer: - b) To control and manage hardware resources

139. Which of the following is a feature of opensource software?

a) It is free to use and can be modified by users

b) It comes with paid licenses

c) It is developed by a single company

d) It is closed source and cannot be modified

Answer: - a) It is free to use and can be modified by users

140. What is the role of utility software in a computer system?

a) To provide entertainment and leisure applications

b) To manage files and perform system maintenance tasks

c) To control hardware components

d) To run user applications

Answer: - b) To manage files and perform system maintenance tasks

141. Which of the following software allows you to edit and manipulate images?

a) Microsoft Word

b) Adobe Photoshop

c) Google Chrome

d) VLC Media Player

Answer: - b) Adobe Photoshop

142. Which of the following is NOT a characteristic of proprietary software?

a) Source code is closed and cannot be modified

b) The software is licensed, and users must pay for it

c) The software is free for anyone to use and modify

d) The developer provides support and updates

Answer: - c) The software is free for anyone to use and modify

143. What is the primary purpose of a web browser?

a) To manage files on the computer

b) To create documents and spreadsheets

c) To browse the internet

d) To process video and audio files

Answer: - c) To browse the internet

144. Which of the following is a common input device for digital audio?

a) Microphone

b) Speaker

c) Printer

d) Monitor

Answer: - a) Microphone

145. Which of the following is used to display the output of a computer?

a) Keyboard

b) Monitor

c) Mouse

d) Scanner

Answer: - b) Monitor

146. Which type of software is most commonly used to browse the internet?

a) Web Browser

b) Word Processor

c) Antivirus Software

d) Spreadsheet Software

Answer: - a) Web Browser

147. What is the primary difference between system software and application software?

a) System software is used for specific tasks, while application software manages hardware

b) System software runs the computer hardware, while application software allows the user to perform tasks

c) System software is more expensive than application software

d) Application software interacts directly with hardware, while system software does not

Answer: - b) System software runs the computer hardware, while application software allows the user to perform tasks

148. Which of the following is an example of secondary storage?

a) ROM

b) Cache

c) SolidState Drive (SSD)

d) RAM

Answer: - c) SolidState Drive (SSD)

149. Which of the following is an example of cloud storage?

a) Google Drive

b) Hard Disk Drive (HDD)

c) Flash Drive

d) Optical Disc

Answer: - a) Google Drive

150. Which of the following is NOT an input device?

a) Mouse

b) Scanner

c) Keyboard

d) Speaker

Answer: - d) Speaker

151. What is the main purpose of the Graphics Processing Unit (GPU)?

a) To execute basic instructions

b) To manage the motherboard

c) To render graphics, videos, and animations

d) To store data permanently

Answer: - c) To render graphics, videos, and animations

152. Which of the following is an example of a utility software?

a) Web Browser

b) Disk Cleanup Tool

c) Spreadsheet Software

d) Video Player

Answer: - b) Disk Cleanup Tool

153. Which of the following is used to connect the computer to a local network or the internet?

a) Hard Disk

b) Network Interface Card (NIC)

c) GPU

d) RAM

Answer: - b) Network Interface Card (NIC)

154. Which of the following storage devices uses laser technology to read data?

a) SSD

b) HDD

c) Optical Disc

d) Flash Drive

Answer: - c) Optical Disc

155. What type of storage device is commonly used to transfer data between computers?

a) SSD

b) Optical Disc

c) USB Flash Drive

d) RAM

Answer: - c) USB Flash Drive

156. What is the main function of an operating system?

a) To display content on the monitor

b) To provide security and antivirus protection

c) To manage hardware and software resources

d) To run applications and games

Answer: - c) To manage hardware and software resources

157. Which of the following is NOT a type of input device?

a) Keyboard

b) Microphone

c) Printer

d) Camera

Answer: - c) Printer

158. What is the role of the Central Processing Unit (CPU) in a computer?

a) To store files

b) To control the flow of data between components

c) To execute instructions and perform calculations

d) To provide power to the system

Answer: - c) To execute instructions and perform calculations

159. Which of the following is NOT a type of system software?

a) Antivirus Software

b) Operating System

c) Device Driver

d) Word Processor

Answer: - d) Word Processor

160. What is the function of RAM in a computer system?

a) To store data permanently

b) To temporarily store data for the CPU to access quickly

c) To manage input and output operations

d) To control the communication between the CPU and other devices

Answer: - b) To temporarily store data for the CPU to access quickly

161. Which of the following is an example of a cloud storage service?

a) Google Drive

b) External Hard Drive

c) Flash Drive

d) CD

Answer: - a) Google Drive

162. Which of the following is a function of a motherboard?

a) To store data

b) To connect and allow communication between all components of the computer

c) To display output on the screen

d) To process instructions and calculations

Answer: - b) To connect and allow communication between all components of the computer

163. What does the term "volatility" refer to in relation to memory?

a) The ability to store data permanently

b) The speed at which data is read and written

c) The loss of data when the power is turned off

d) The physical size of the memory chip

Answer: - c) The loss of data when the power is turned off

164. Which of the following is a type of output device?

a) Scanner

b) Monitor

c) Keyboard

d) Microphone

Answer: - b) Monitor

165. Which of the following is a type of secondary storage device?

a) RAM

b) Hard Disk Drive (HDD)

c) CPU

d) Cache Memory

Answer: - b) Hard Disk Drive (HDD)

166. Which of the following is an example of proprietary software?

a) Linux

b) Mozilla Firefox

c) Adobe Photoshop

d) LibreOffice

Answer: - c) Adobe Photoshop

167. What is the main advantage of using opensource software?

a) It is easy to use

b) It is free and customizable

c) It is more secure than proprietary software

d) It is always preinstalled on computers

Answer: - b) It is free and customizable

168. Which of the following is a function of the Arithmetic Logic Unit (ALU) in the CPU?

a) To control data flow within the computer

b) To perform mathematical and logical operations

c) To execute program instructions

d) To store data for later use

Answer: - b) To perform mathematical and logical operations

169. Which of the following software is used for realtime communication over the internet?

a) Zoom

b) Microsoft Word

c) VLC Media Player

d) Google Chrome

Answer: - a) Zoom

170. Which of the following storage devices is the fastest?

a) Hard Disk Drive (HDD)

b) SolidState Drive (SSD)

c) Optical Disc

d) Flash Drive

Answer: - b) SolidState Drive (SSD)

171. Which of the following is a main feature of Linux?

a) It is a proprietary software

b) It is highly customizable and opensource

c) It is only used for gaming

d) It is not compatible with hardware devices

Answer: - b) It is highly customizable and opensource

172. Which of the following software is used for spreadsheet creation?

a) Microsoft Word

b) Microsoft Excel

c) Microsoft PowerPoint

d) Adobe Acrobat

Answer: - b) Microsoft Excel

173. Which of the following is an example of a device that uses optical storage?

a) USB Flash Drive

b) Hard Disk Drive (HDD)

c) CD/DVD

d) RAM

Answer: - c) CD/DVD

174. What type of memory is used in SolidState Drives (SSDs)?

a) Magnetic

b) Flash memory

c) Optical

d) Dynamic RAM

Answer: - b) Flash memory

175. Which of the following is an example of a specialized processing unit used for rendering graphics?

a) CPU

b) GPU

c) RAM

d) Motherboard

Answer: - b) GPU

176. What is the main purpose of using a printer in a computer system?

a) To store data

b) To produce hard copies of digital documents

c) To display images

d) To process data

Answer: - b) To produce hard copies of digital documents

177. What is the primary function of a computer's cooling system?

a) To clean the computer

b) To maintain optimal operating temperature for components

c) To increase processing speed

d) To store data

Answer: - b) To maintain optimal operating temperature for components

178. What is an example of an external storage device?

a) CPU

b) RAM

c) External Hard Drive

d) SSD

Answer: - c) External Hard Drive

179. Which of the following is NOT an operating system?

a) Windows

b) macOS

c) Linux

d) Google Chrome

Answer: - d) Google Chrome

180. What is the primary function of a device driver?

a) To help software run faster

b) To control peripheral devices connected to the computer

c) To protect against malware

d) To store data permanently

Answer: - b) To control peripheral devices connected to the computer

181. Which of the following is a type of application software?

a) Operating System

b) Disk Cleanup Tool

c) Web Browser

d) Device Driver

Answer: - c) Web Browser

182. What is the primary function of the motherboard in a computer?

a) To store data

b) To perform calculations

c) To connect all components and allow them to communicate

d) To display output on the screen

Answer: - c) To connect all components and allow them to communicate

183. Which of the following is a nonvolatile storage device?

a) RAM

b) Hard Disk Drive (HDD)

c) Cache Memory

d) CPU

Answer: - b) Hard Disk Drive (HDD)

184. What does the term “cloud storage” refer to?

a) Storing data in physical external drives

b) Storing data on remote servers accessible via the internet

c) Storing data in the computer’s internal hard drive

d) Storing data in a local area network

Answer: - b) Storing data on remote servers accessible via the internet

185. Which type of operating system is designed to be opensource and free to use?

a) Windows

b) macOS

c) Linux

d) Android

Answer: - c) Linux

186. Which of the following is the most commonly used input device?

a) Microphone

b) Keyboard

c) Monitor

d) Printer

Answer: - b) Keyboard

187. Which of the following is an example of secondary storage?

a) RAM

b) SSD

c) CPU

d) Cache Memory

Answer: - b) SSD

188. What is the primary advantage of solidstate drives (SSDs) over hard disk drives (HDDs)?

a) Larger storage capacity

b) Faster read and write speeds

c) Lower cost

d) Higher durability

Answer: - b) Faster read and write speeds

189. Which of the following is NOT an example of an output device?

a) Printer

b) Monitor

c) Speaker

d) Scanner

Answer: - d) Scanner

190. What is the function of the Arithmetic Logic Unit (ALU) in the CPU?

a) To perform logical and arithmetic operations

b) To store data

c) To manage input and output

d) To execute software applications

Answer: - a) To perform logical and arithmetic operations

191. Which of the following software types helps manage and maintain the computer's hardware?

a) Operating System

b) Antivirus Software

c) Web Browser

d) Media Player

Answer: - a) Operating System

192. What is the purpose of using a graphics card in a computer?

a) To increase storage capacity

b) To process and render images and videos

c) To connect to the internet

d) To manage system memory

Answer: - b) To process and render images and videos

193. Which of the following is a key feature of proprietary software?

a) Free to use and modify

b) Can be redistributed by users

c) The source code is closed and owned by a specific entity

d) Supported by opensource communities

Answer: - c) The source code is closed and owned by a specific entity

194. Which of the following operating systems is developed by Apple?

a) Windows

b) macOS

c) Linux

d) Android

Answer: - b) macOS

195. What is the primary function of a disk cleanup tool?

a) To check for viruses

b) To free up space on the hard drive by deleting unnecessary files

c) To speed up the CPU

d) To backup data

Answer: - b) To free up space on the hard drive by deleting unnecessary files

196. Which of the following is a type of peripheral device?

a) CPU

b) Monitor

c) Cache

d) RAM

Answer: - b) Monitor

197. Which of the following is a type of software that helps protect a computer from malware and viruses?

a) Antivirus Software

b) Word Processor

c) Spreadsheet Software

d) Web Browser

Answer: - a) Antivirus Software

198. What does the term "volatile memory" refer to in relation to a computer's storage?

a) Memory that retains data even when the computer is powered off

b) Memory that stores data temporarily and loses it when the power is off

c) Memory that is readonly

d) Memory that is used to process data

Answer: - b) Memory that stores data temporarily and loses it when the power is off

199. Which of the following is an advantage of using a web browser?

a) It helps process data

b) It stores data permanently

c) It allows users to access websites on the internet

d) It increases storage space

Answer: - c) It allows users to access websites on the internet

200. Which of the following is a type of application software that helps users create and edit text documents?

a) Google Docs

b) Microsoft Word

c) LibreOffice

d) All of the above

Answer: - d) All of the above

Types of Number Systems

1. Which number system is the most fundamental in computing?

A) Decimal

B) Octal

C) Binary

D) Hexadecimal

Answer: - C

2. The binary number system consists of which two digits?

A) 1 and 2

B) 0 and 1

C) 0 and 9

D) 2 and 3

Answer: - B

3. Why do computers operate on binary?

A) It is easier for humans to read.

B) Digital circuits recognize two states: - on (1) and off (0).

C) It requires less storage space.

D) Binary is a universal language.

Answer: - B

4. Which number system is most commonly used by humans?

A) Binary

B) Octal

C) Hexadecimal

D) Decimal

Answer: - D

5. What is the base of the octal number system?

A) 2

B) 8

C) 10

D) 16

Answer: - B

6. Which symbols are used in the hexadecimal system?

A) 09 and AZ

B) 09 and AF

C) AF only

D) 015

Answer: - B

7. How many binary digits correspond to one hexadecimal digit?

A) 2

B) 3

C) 4

D) 8

Answer: - C

8. The octal number system is a shorthand for which number system?

A) Decimal

B) Hexadecimal

C) Binary

D) None of the above

Answer: - C

9. What is the binary equivalent of decimal 10?

A) 1001

B) 1100

C) 1010

D) 1110

Answer: - C

10. The hexadecimal equivalent of binary 1111 is: -

A) E

B) F

C) 15

D) 10

Answer: - B

Conversions Between Number Systems

11. What is the first step in converting a decimal number to binary?

A) Multiply by 2

B) Divide by 2

C) Add 2

D) Subtract 2

Answer: - B

12. In decimal to binary conversion, what is done with the remainders?

A) Write them in order.

B) Discard them.

C) Write them in reverse order.

D) Multiply them.

Answer: - C

13. The binary equivalent of decimal 5 is: -

A) 100

B) 101

C) 110

D) 111

Answer: - B

14. To convert binary to decimal, you: -

A) Divide by 2 repeatedly.

B) Add all the binary digits directly.

C) Multiply each binary digit by powers of 2 and add.

D) Multiply each binary digit by powers of 10 and subtract.

Answer: - C

15. The octal equivalent of binary 110 is: -

A) 5

B) 6

C) 7

D) 8

Answer: - B

16. The hexadecimal equivalent of binary 1010 is: -

A) 8

B) 9

C) A

D) B

Answer: - C

17. What is the binary equivalent of hexadecimal A3?

A) 10100010

B) 10100011

C) 10101100

D) 10100111

Answer: - B

18. How do you convert decimal 65 to octal?

A) Divide by 2

B) Divide by 8

C) Divide by 16

D) Divide by 10

Answer: - B

19. What is the octal equivalent of decimal 65?

A) 100

B) 101

C) 110

D) 111

Answer: - B

20. The binary equivalent of hexadecimal FF is: -

A) 11111110

B) 11111111

C) 10101010

D) 11001100

Answer: - B

21. Which number system is used for digital circuit operations?

A) Decimal

B) Binary

C) Octal

D) Hexadecimal

Answer: - B

22. Why is hexadecimal used in programming?

A) It is easier for computers to process.

B) It simplifies binary representation for humans.

C) It uses fewer digits than binary.

D) Both B and C.

Answer: - D

23. What is measured in binary units like KB, MB, and GB?

A) Time

B) Storage and memory

C) Distance

D) Network speed

Answer: - B

24. IP addresses in computer networks are often represented in which system?

A) Decimal

B) Binary

C) Hexadecimal

D) All of the above

Answer: - D

25. What role do number systems play in error detection?

A) None

B) Simplify network addresses

C) Create reliable algorithms for data transmission

D) Reduce data processing time

Answer: - C

26. What is the hexadecimal equivalent of decimal 255?

A) FE

B) 1F

C) FF

D) 100

Answer: - C

27. How many digits are in the base8 (octal) system?

A) 8

B) 10

C) 16

D) 2

Answer: - A

28. Which binary value represents decimal 15?

A) 1100

B) 1111

C) 1010

D) 1001

Answer: - B

29. What is the octal equivalent of decimal 8?

A) 8

B) 10

C) 11

D) 12

Answer: - B

30. Convert binary 1001 to hexadecimal: -

A) 8

B) 9

C) A

D) B

Answer: - B

31. Which system simplifies debugging in low level programming?

A) Decimal

B) Binary

C) Hexadecimal

D) Octal

Answer: - C

32. The binary value of hexadecimal ‘C’ is: -

A) 1000

B) 1010

C) 1100

D) 1111

Answer: - C

33. What is the hexadecimal equivalent of binary 101010?

A) 2A

B) 2F

C) 1A

D) 1F

Answer: - A

34. The octal equivalent of binary 101001 is: -

A) 51

B) 61

C) 71

D) 111

Answer: - A

35. The decimal equivalent of hexadecimal '1F' is: -

A) 31

B) 30

C) 15

D) 16

Answer: - A

36. Which number system is essential for memory addressing?

A) Decimal

B) Binary

C) Hexadecimal

D) Octal

Answer: - C

37. How does the binary system assist in data representation?

A) Converts data into easy to read decimal values.

B) Enables data to be processed by digital circuits.

C) Helps reduce data redundancy.

D) Stores data as hexadecimal for computation.

Answer: - B

38. What is one advantage of using the octal system in computing?

A) Fewer digits than binary.

B) Higher precision than hexadecimal.

C) Directly compatible with ASCII.

D) Easier to process than decimal.

Answer: - A

39. Which number system is used to represent colors in digital systems?

A) Decimal

B) Octal

C) Binary

D) Hexadecimal

Answer: - D

40. Why are MAC addresses written in hexadecimal?

A) Compact and easier to understand.

B) Directly translatable into octal.

C) Uses more memory.

D) Faster for processors to interpret.

Answer: - A

41. In which number system is file size most commonly represented?

A) Binary

B) Decimal

C) Octal

D) Hexadecimal

Answer: - A

42. What is the purpose of error detection algorithms?

A) Reduce processing power.

B) Ensure reliable data transmission.

C) Increase memory usage.

D) Convert hexadecimal to binary.

Answer: - B

43. Which system is often used in IP addressing?

A) Decimal

B) Binary

C) Both A and B

D) Hexadecimal only

Answer: - C

44. Which type of number system is primarily used in assembly language?

A) Decimal

B) Octal

C) Hexadecimal

D) Binary

Answer: - C

45. What is the main reason binary is ideal for digital circuits?

A) It supports fast addition.

B) It uses only two states.

C) It is human readable.

D) It occupies less space.

Answer: - B

46. Convert decimal 100 to binary: -

A) 1111100

B) 1100100

C) 1010100

D) 1110000

Answer: - B

47. Convert binary 11110000 to decimal: -

A) 224

B) 240

C) 192

D) 128

Answer: - B

48. Convert octal 74 to decimal: -

A) 60

B) 62

C) 58

D) 60

Answer: - D

49. What is the binary equivalent of octal 17?

A) 10111

B) 1111

C) 11111

D) 11101

Answer: - A

50. Convert hexadecimal 2C to binary: -

A) 111000

B) 101100

C) 111100

D) 110110

Answer: - B

51. Which number system is most commonly used for color coding in HTML?

A) Binary

B) Octal

C) Hexadecimal

D) Decimal

Answer: - C

52. How many bits are used in a MAC address?

A) 16

B) 32

C) 48

D) 64

Answer: - C

53. Convert binary 10101 to octal: -

A) 21

B) 25

C) 15

D) 11

Answer: - D

54. What is the hexadecimal representation of binary 11100011?

A) E3

B) D3

C) F3

D) A3

Answer: - A

55. Convert decimal 85 to hexadecimal: -

A) 51

B) 55

C) 85

D) 59

Answer: - A

91. What is the binary equivalent of decimal 1024?

A) 10000000

B) 110000000

C) 10000000000

D) 10100000000

Answer: - C

92. What is the hexadecimal representation of binary 11011010?

A) DA

B) D9

C) DB

D) CA

Answer: - A

93. Convert decimal 255 to octal: -

A) 375

B) 377

C) 376

D) 374

Answer: - B

94. Which number system is used to represent colors in web design?

A) Binary

B) Hexadecimal

C) Octal

D) Decimal

Answer: - B

95. The decimal equivalent of octal 123 is: -

A) 83

B) 81

C) 82

D) 80

Answer: - A

96. Convert hexadecimal 1F4 to decimal: -

A) 490

B) 494

C) 500

D) 504

Answer: - C

97. What is the binary representation of octal 64?

A) 110010

B) 111010

C) 100110

D) 101010

Answer: - A

98. Convert binary 10000001 to decimal: -

A) 129

B) 130

C) 127

D) 128

Answer: - A

99. What is the primary use of the octal number system in modern computing?

A) Representing binary data compactly.

B) Memory addressing in computers.

C) Defining file permissions in UNIX systems.

D) Simplifying hexadecimal numbers.

Answer: - C

100. What is the hexadecimal equivalent of decimal 500?

A) 1FA

B) 1F3

C) 1F4

D) 1FB

Answer: - C

Basic Concepts logic gates

1. What are logic gates used for?

A) Storing data

B) Performing logical operations

C) Generating electricity

D) Controlling traffic lights

Answer: - B

2. Logic gates operate using which type of logic?

A) Decimal logic

B) Binary logic

C) Octal logic

D) Hexadecimal logic

Answer: - B

3. What does binary logic consist of?

A) Three states: - 1, 0, 1

B) Two states: - 0 and 1

C) Four states: - 0, 1, 2, 3

D) Two states: - on and off only

Answer: - B

4. Which of the following is NOT a primary logic gate?

A) AND

B) XOR

C) NOT

D) BUFFER

Answer: - D

5. What is the symbol of an AND gate?

A) Flatended shape

B) Curved shape

C) Triangle with a circle

D) Rectangle

Answer: - A

6. When does an AND gate output 1?

A) When all inputs are 0

B) When all inputs are 1

C) When at least one input is 1

D) When inputs are different

Answer: - B

7. What is the output of an AND gate if inputs are A=1, B=0?

A) 0

B) 1

C) Undefined

D) Same as input A

Answer: - A

8. Where is an AND gate typically used?

A) Alarm systems

B) Security systems requiring multiple conditions to be met

C) Remote controls

D) Traffic lights

Answer: - B

9. What is the function of an OR gate?

A) Outputs 1 only when all inputs are 1

B) Outputs 1 if at least one input is 1

C) Outputs the opposite of the input

D) Outputs 0 if inputs are 1

Answer: - B

10. What is the symbol of an OR gate?

A) Curved shape

B) Triangle with a circle

C) Flatended shape

D) Curved shape with a circle

Answer: - A

11. What is the output of an OR gate if inputs are A=0, B=1?

A) 0

B) 1

C) Undefined

D) Same as input A

Answer: - B

12. Which of the following uses an OR gate?

A) Traffic light systems

B) Systems that require any condition to trigger an action

C) Security systems

D) Memory storage devices

Answer: - B

13. What is the function of a NOT gate?

A) Outputs 1 when inputs are 1

B) Outputs 0 when inputs are 1

C) Inverts the input

D) Combines inputs

Answer: - C

14. What is the symbol of a NOT gate?

A) Flatended shape

B) Triangle with a circle

C) Curved shape

D) Rectangle

Answer: - B

15. What is the output of a NOT gate if input is 1?

A) 0

B) 1

C) Undefined

D) Depends on other inputs

Answer: - A

16. Where is a NOT gate commonly used?

A) Security systems

B) Inverting signals in circuits

C) Arithmetic calculations

D) Signal amplifiers

Answer: - B

17. What is the function of a NAND gate?

A) Outputs 1 only when all inputs are 1

B) Outputs 0 only when all inputs are 1

C) Outputs 1 when inputs are 0

D) Combines inputs to give the sum

Answer: - B

18. What is unique about a NAND gate?

A) It is used for low power circuits

B) It can be used to create any other gate

C) It has no applications in real world systems

D) It requires multiple outputs

Answer: - B

19. What is the output of a NAND gate if inputs are A=1, B=1?

A) 0

B) 1

C) Undefined

D) Same as input A

Answer: - A

20. Where are NAND gates commonly used?

A) Traffic light systems

B) Memory storage elements

C) Remote controls

D) Signal processing circuits

Answer: - B

21. What is the function of a NOR gate?

A) Outputs 1 when at least one input is 1

B) Outputs 1 only when all inputs are 0

C) Outputs the same as the input

D) Inverts the input

Answer: - B

22. What is the symbol of a NOR gate?

A) Curved shape with a circle

B) Flatended shape

C) Triangle with a circle

D) Rectangle

Answer: - A

23. What is the output of a NOR gate if inputs are A=0, B=0?

A) 0

B) 1

C) Undefined

D) Same as input A

Answer: - B

24. Which system uses NOR gates?

A) Alarm systems

B) Digital comparators

C) Memory storage elements

D) Parity checkers

Answer: - A

25. What is the function of an XOR gate?

A) Outputs 1 only when all inputs are 1

B) Outputs 1 if only one input is 1

C) Outputs 0 when inputs are the same

D) Outputs 1 when both inputs are 0

Answer: - B

26. What is the symbol of an XOR gate?

A) Triangle with a circle

B) Flatended shape

C) Curved shape with an additional line

D) Rectangle

Answer: - C

27. What is the output of an XOR gate if inputs are A=1, B=1?

A) 1

B) 0

C) Undefined

D) Same as input A

Answer: - B

28. Where are XOR gates commonly used?

A) Equality detectors

B) Systems requiring toggling functions

C) Memory elements

D) Alarm systems

Answer: - B

29. What is the function of an XNOR gate?

A) Outputs 1 only when inputs are the same

B) Outputs 0 only when inputs are different

C) Outputs 1 when all inputs are 1

D) Inverts the input

Answer: - A

30. What is the symbol of an XNOR gate?

A) Curved shape with a circle

B) Curved shape with an additional line and a circle

C) Flatended shape

D) Rectangle

Answer: - B

31. What is the output of an XNOR gate if inputs are A=1, B=0?

A) 0

B) 1

C) Undefined

D) Same as input A

Answer: - A

32. Where are XNOR gates commonly used?

A) Parity checkers and digital comparators

B) Systems requiring toggling functions

C) Alarm systems

D) Arithmetic circuits

Answer: - A

33. What is a truth table used for?

A) To describe how circuits are connected

B) To determine a logic gate's output for all input combinations

C) To design the physical layout of circuits

D) To measure power consumption of gates

Answer: - B

34. Which gate's truth table has all outputs 0 except for the case where both inputs are 1?

A) AND

B) OR

C) NOT

D) NAND

Answer: - A

35. What do the rows in a truth table represent?

A) Physical circuits

B) Possible input combinations

C) Output voltages

D) Circuit diagrams

Answer: - B

36. How many rows are needed in a truth table for a 3input gate?

A) 4

B) 6

C) 8

D) 12

Answer: - C

37. Which logic gate is commonly used in security systems requiring multiple conditions?

A) AND

B) OR

C) NAND

D) XOR

Answer: - A

38. Which logic gate is used in alarm systems that activate only when no inputs are active?

A) NAND

B) NOR

C) AND

D) XOR

Answer: - B

39. In digital circuits, which gate can function as a universal gate?

A) AND

B) NAND

C) OR

D) XNOR

Answer: - B

40. What type of gates are used in equality detectors?

A) AND

B) XOR

C) XNOR

D) NOR

Answer: - C

41. What is a key application of XOR gates?

A) Decoding signals

B) Checking parity in communication systems

C) Memory storage

D) Amplifying signals

Answer: - B

42. Which component in a CPU uses logic gates to decode instructions?

A) Memory unit

B) Control unit

C) Arithmetic Logic Unit (ALU)

D) Input devices

Answer: - B

43. What role do logic gates play in memory storage?

A) Store binary data using flipflops

B) Decode instructions for storage devices

C) Amplify signals for storage

D) Manage data flow between memory units

Answer: - A

44. Which gate is essential for creating adders in arithmetic operations?

A) AND

B) XOR

C) OR

D) NOT

Answer: - B

45. Digital signal processing often uses logic gates for what purpose?

A) Storing signals

B) Filtering and modulation

C) Measuring signal strength

D) Reversing signals

Answer: - B

46. Which system uses logic gates to control light sequences?

A) Smartphones

B) Traffic lights

C) Washing machines

D) Gaming consoles

Answer: - B

47. How are logic gates used in smartphones?

A) Managing touch screen inputs

B) Decoding TV signals

C) Powering the device

D) Processing analog signals

Answer: - A

48. What do modern cars use logic gates for?

A) Engine management and safety systems

B) Accelerating the vehicle

C) Controlling tire pressure

D) Enhancing fuel efficiency

Answer: - A

49. Gaming consoles rely on logic gates for which purpose?

A) Storing game data

B) Rendering graphics and handling user inputs

C) Decoding audio signals

D) Managing power supply

Answer: - B

50. What combination of gates might be used to manage a traffic light system?

A) AND and OR gates

B) AND and NOT gates

C) NAND and XOR gates

D) NOR and XNOR gates

Answer: - B

51. How many rows are in a truth table for a 4input gate?

A) 8

B) 12

C) 16

D) 32

Answer: - C

52. Which logic gate's truth table shows all outputs as 1 except when all inputs are 1?

A) NAND

B) NOR

C) AND

D) XOR

Answer: - A

53. Which logic gate has the simplest truth table with only two possible outcomes: - an inverse of the input?

A) NOT

B) AND

C) OR

D) NOR

Answer: - A

54. What is the significance of a truth table in logic gate design?

A) It provides a physical layout for the circuit.

B) It defines the behavior of the gate for all input combinations.

C) It predicts power consumption.

D) It measures voltage levels.

Answer: - B

55. Which component in a CPU combines logic gates to perform arithmetic operations?

A) Control Unit

B) Cache Memory

C) Arithmetic Logic Unit (ALU)

D) Register

Answer: - C

56. What type of gate is integral to the design of flipflops used in memory storage?

A) NAND

B) OR

C) XOR

D) NOT

Answer: - A

57. How do logic gates assist in digital signal processing?

A) By storing signals for analysis

B) By enabling error detection and modulation

C) By converting analog signals to digital

D) By boosting signal strength

Answer: - B

58. Which logic gate can be used to create a basic half-adder circuit?

A) AND and OR

B) XOR and AND

C) NAND and OR

D) XOR and NOT

Answer: - B

59. What is the role of XNOR gates in computing?

A) Detecting equality between binary numbers

B) Performing binary addition

C) Controlling circuit power

D) Detecting memory faults

Answer: - A

60. What combination of gates is essential in building a fulladder?

A) AND, OR, and NOT gates

B) XOR, AND, and OR gates

C) NAND and NOR gates

D) XNOR, XOR, and OR gates

Answer: - B

61. How are logic gates used in modern washing machines?

A) To control heating elements

B) To manage program selection and timing

C) To amplify motor signals

D) To ensure power efficiency

Answer: - B

62. Which gate could turn on a light only when both switches A and B are on?

A) AND gate

B) OR gate

C) NAND gate

D) XOR gate

Answer: - A

63. What kind of gate might be used in an automated sprinkler system that activates only if both moisture and temperature sensors are within specific ranges?

A) AND

B) OR

C) NOT

D) NOR

Answer: - A

64. In a remote control system, which logic gate might decode incoming signals?

A) AND gate

B) XOR gate

C) OR gate

D) NOR gate

Answer: - B

65. What logic gate ensures a car's alarm activates only when all sensors detect no movement?

A) NAND

B) NOR

C) AND

D) OR

Answer: - B

66. How are gates used in gaming console circuits?

A) To store user profiles

B) To decode audio signals

C) To execute game logic and render graphics

D) To manage network connectivity

Answer: - C

67. What kind of gates control the sequencing of traffic lights?

A) OR and NOR gates

B) NAND and NOT gates

C) AND and NOT gates

D) XOR and XNOR gates

Answer: - C

68. In home appliances, what role do logic gates play?

A) Managing user inputs and device functions

B) Amplifying electronic signals

C) Storing operational data

D) Enhancing power efficiency

Answer: - A

69. Which gate is likely to be used in a touch sensitive smartphone circuit?

A) OR gate

B) NAND gate

C) XOR gate

D) AND gate

Answer: - C

70. What logic gates are used in calculators for binary addition?

A) NAND and NOR

B) XOR and AND

C) OR and NOT

D) XNOR and XOR

Answer: - B

71. What makes NAND and NOR gates “universal” gates?

A) They consume less power.

B) They can be used to construct all other gates.

C) They require fewer inputs.

D) They are faster than other gates.

Answer: - B

72. Which logic gate is best for creating a signal inverter?

A) AND

B) NOT

C) OR

D) NAND

Answer: - B

73. What is the main difference between an OR gate and an XOR gate?

A) XOR outputs 0 when inputs are the same; OR outputs 1.

B) XOR uses 3 inputs; OR uses 2.

C) OR gates consume more power.

D) XOR gates have a faster response time.

Answer: - A

74. How do NOT gates contribute to more complex circuits?

A) By reducing signal power

B) By creating inverted outputs

C) By enhancing other gate signals

D) By decoding binary signals

Answer: - B

75. Which gates are used in systems where multiple conditions must be false to activate an output?

A) AND and OR

B) NAND and NOR

C) XOR and XNOR

D) NOT and NOR

Answer: - B

76. Which gate is most suitable for toggling operations in circuits?

A) AND

B) OR

C) XOR

D) NOR

Answer: - C

77. How can you build a NOT gate using a universal NAND gate?

A) Connect one input to 1 and the other to the signal.

B) Connect both inputs to the same signal.

C) Use three NAND gates in series.

D) Connect one input to 0 and the other to the signal.

Answer: - B

78. What is the primary difference between a NAND gate and an AND gate?

A) NAND gate outputs are always 0.

B) NAND gate outputs are the inverse of an AND gate's outputs.

C) NAND gates use more power.

D) NAND gates require fewer inputs.

Answer: - B

79. Which gate is often referred to as a "comparator" in digital circuits?

A) XOR

B) AND

C) XNOR

D) NOR

Answer: - C

80. What combination of gates can replace an OR gate?

A) Two XOR gates

B) Two NAND gates

C) One NAND gate and one NOT gate

D) Two NOR gates and one NOT gate

Answer: - D

81. What type of logic gate is crucial in flipflops, the building blocks of memory storage?

A) XOR

B) NAND

C) AND

D) OR

Answer: - B

82. How do XNOR gates assist in error checking systems?

A) By ensuring all inputs are high

B) By comparing input signals to verify equality

C) By inverting error signals

D) By reducing binary input values

Answer: - B

83. In digital comparators, which gate detects inequality between two binary numbers?

A) XOR

B) XNOR

C) OR

D) NAND

Answer: - A

84. What gates are frequently used in traffic light sequencing to avoid signal overlap?

A) AND and NOT

B) OR and NAND

C) NOR and XOR

D) XNOR and AND

Answer: - A

85. Which logic gate is used in alarm systems to activate the alarm when any single input condition is met?

A) XOR

B) OR

C) AND

D) NOR

Answer: - B

86. How does the XOR gate contribute to cryptographic systems?

A) By storing encryption keys

B) By toggling between input signals

C) By ensuring exclusive input combinations for encryption

D) By comparing encryption states

Answer: - C

87. Which gate combination would allow a green traffic light only when the opposite red light is on?

A) NOT gate

B) AND gate

C) NAND gate

D) OR gate

Answer: - A

88. In gaming consoles, how are logic gates primarily utilized?

A) Storing data temporarily

B) Executing game logic and rendering graphics

C) Enhancing audiovisual output

D) Managing network communication

Answer: - B

89. What gates are involved in basic memory storage circuits like latches?

A) NAND and NOR

B) XOR and XNOR

C) OR and NOT

D) AND and OR

Answer: - A

90. How does the NOT gate assist in a thermostat circuit?

A) By amplifying temperature signals

B) By inverting the temperature sensor output for heating/cooling decisions

C) By reducing power consumption

D) By enhancing cooling functions

Answer: - B

91. What is the key advantage of using universal gates in circuit design?

A) They can mimic all other gates.

B) They are more energy efficient.

C) They simplify circuit diagrams.

D) They require fewer inputs.

Answer: - A

92. Which gate is used to construct a simple parity checker?

A) XOR

B) OR

C) NAND

D) NOR

Answer: - A

93. How can you design a halfadder using logic gates?

A) Using XOR and AND gates

B) Using NAND and NOR gates

C) Using OR and NOT gates

D) Using XOR and NOR gates

Answer: - A

94. What is the role of truth tables in digital circuit design?

A) Analyzing power consumption

B) Representing all possible input output combinations

C) Simplifying circuit complexity

D) Predicting signal delay

Answer: - B

95. Which gates can form the basis of a full adder circuit?

A) XOR, AND, and OR

B) NAND, OR, and NOT

C) XNOR and XOR

D) AND and OR

Answer: - A

96. How is a NOR gate used to implement a NOT gate?

A) By connecting both inputs to the same signal

B) By connecting one input to a fixed 1

C) By using two NOR gates in series

D) By connecting the output back to the input

Answer: - A

97. What kind of logic gate ensures the output remains high unless all inputs are active?

A) OR gate

B) NAND gate

C) NOR gate

D) AND gate

Answer: - B

98. In a binary addition circuit, what logic gates handle the carryout operation?

A) AND and OR gates

B) XOR and NOT gates

C) AND and XOR gates

D) NAND and NOR gates

Answer: - C

99. What is the primary use of a logic gate in a decoder circuit?

A) To amplify the input signals

B) To convert binary codes into corresponding outputs

C) To store data temporarily

D) To execute arithmetic calculations

Answer: - B

100. Which gate configuration can replace a NOR gate using only NAND gates?

A) Two NAND gates with one inverted output

B) Four NAND gates with a NOT inverter

C) Three NAND gates with both inputs connected

D) Five NAND gates in sequence

Answer: - B

Operating systems

1. What is an Operating System (OS)?

A) A type of application software

B) A system that only handles the CPU

C) Software that manages hardware and software resources

D) A hardware component that controls the computer

Answer: - C

2. Which of the following is NOT a key characteristic of an OS?

A) Resource Management

B) Program Execution

C) Directly controlling applications

D) Security and Protection

Answer: - C

3. What is the primary role of an Operating System?

A) Convert applications into hardware

B) Manage system resources and provide a platform for applications

C) Perform only arithmetic calculations

D) Translate programming languages

Answer: - B

4. Without an OS, users would need to interact with hardware using what?

A) Graphical interfaces

B) Command prompts

C) Complex machine language

D) Application shortcuts

Answer: - C

5. What is the role of the user interface in an OS?

A) Manages files

B) Provides interaction between the user and the system

C) Handles security protocols

D) Optimizes application performance

Answer: - B

6. Which of the following tasks is related to resource management by an OS?

A) Securing internet connections

B) Allocating CPU time and memory to processes

C) Managing software installation

D) Updating drivers automatically

Answer: - B

7. Which OS characteristic protects data and system resources from unauthorized access?

A) User Interface

B) Program Execution

C) Security and Protection

D) Resource Management

Answer: - C

8. What does process management in an OS involve?

A) Handling memory allocation

B) Executing, scheduling, and synchronizing processes

C) Establishing network connections

D) Managing user passwords

Answer: - B

9. Which of the following is NOT a responsibility of process management?

A) Multitasking

B) Interprocess Communication (IPC)

C) Memory Protection

D) Process Scheduling

Answer: - C

10. What is multitasking in an OS?

A) Performing a single task repeatedly

B) Allowing multiple processes to run by switching between them rapidly

C) Running multiple systems simultaneously

D) Controlling a single process in different ways

Answer: - B

11. Which function of the OS ensures processes don't interfere with each other?

A) Memory Allocation

B) Process Scheduling

C) Process Synchronization

D) I/O Management

Answer: - C

12. What does memory management NOT include?

A) Allocating and deallocating memory

B) Managing virtual memory

C) Managing passwords

D) Protecting memory access

Answer: - C

13. What is virtual memory?

A) Memory allocated to specific users

B) A method that uses a portion of the hard drive as RAM

C) Temporary storage for caching files

D) Memory used only for gaming

Answer: - B

14. What role does memory protection play in an OS?

A) Prevents unauthorized users from accessing files

B) Ensures data integrity by isolating process memory

C) Allocates equal memory to all processes

D) Protects hardware components from damage

Answer: - B

15. Which of the following is NOT part of I/O management?

A) Device communication

B) Buffering and caching

C) Process scheduling

D) Handling device drivers

Answer: - C

16. What is the primary purpose of device drivers in an OS?

A) Translate user commands into machine code

B) Allow the OS to communicate with hardware devices

C) Secure the system from malware

D) Run applications faster

Answer: - B

17. What is buffering in I/O management?

A) Temporarily storing data to improve efficiency

B) Clearing all memory after execution

C) Executing programs directly from RAM

D) Interpreting user commands

Answer: - A

18. What type of OS executes jobs sequentially without user interaction?

A) Batch Operating System

B) RealTime Operating System

C) Distributed Operating System

D) Timesharing Operating System

Answer: - A

19. Which OS allows multiple users to access the system simultaneously?

A) Batch OS

B) TimeSharing OS

C) RealTime OS

D) Embedded OS

Answer: - B

20. What is a major feature of distributed operating systems?

A) They allow hardware devices to share resources directly.

B) They operate as if running on a single unified system.

C) They are used only in robotics.

D) They do not require memory management.

Answer: - B

21. Which of the following is NOT a characteristic of a batch operating system?

A) Processes jobs in bulk

B) Does not require direct user interaction

C) Provides real-time task execution

D) Suitable for tasks with similar requirements

Answer: - C

22. Timesharing operating systems improve CPU efficiency by using what method?

A) Job grouping

B) Time slicing

C) Batch execution

D) Parallel processing

Answer: - B

23. Which type of OS is best suited for handling tasks that require immediate response?

A) Batch Operating System

B) Distributed Operating System

C) RealTime Operating System

D) TimeSharing Operating System

Answer: - C

24. What is an example of a RealTime Operating System (RTOS)?

A) Android

B) UNIX

C) VxWorks

D) Windows 10

Answer: - C

25. Which OS type allows resource sharing across multiple connected systems?

A) Distributed Operating System

B) Batch Operating System

C) TimeSharing Operating System

D) RealTime Operating System

Answer: - A

26. What is the primary purpose of virtual memory in an OS?

A) Increase CPU speed

B) Allow programs larger than physical memory to run

C) Secure memory from unauthorized access

D) Manage I/O devices

Answer: - B

27. Which component of an OS is responsible for scheduling tasks?

A) Memory Manager

B) Process Scheduler

C) Device Driver

D) File System

Answer: - B

28. In a timesharing OS, what ensures multiple users feel they have exclusive access?

A) Device drivers

B) Virtual memory

C) Time slicing

D) Batch processing

Answer: - C

29. What does "multitasking" in an OS allow?

A) Running multiple programs simultaneously

B) Running a single program at maximum speed

C) Sharing I/O devices across systems

D) Executing batch processes in realtime

Answer: - A

30. What ensures data integrity when multiple processes share resources?

A) Buffering

B) Process Synchronization

C) Virtual Memory

D) Time Slicing

Answer: - B

31. What is a critical feature of RealTime Operating Systems?

A) Delayed response times

B) Predictable and immediate task execution

C) Batch processing capabilities

D) High resource consumption

Answer: - B

32. Which type of OS is best suited for embedded systems and robotics?

A) Distributed Operating System

B) TimeSharing Operating System

C) RealTime Operating System

D) Batch Operating System

Answer: - C

33. What is the primary role of the kernel in an OS?

A) Provides a userfriendly interface

B) Manages core system resources

C) Handles application installation

D) Controls external hardware only

Answer: - B

34. Which type of OS is used in scientific research requiring high fault tolerance?

A) Batch Operating System

B) TimeSharing Operating System

C) Distributed Operating System

D) Embedded Operating System

Answer: - C

35. What is the main feature of UNIX as an OS?

A) Realtime responsiveness

B) Userfriendly graphical interface

C) Multiuser and multitasking capabilities

D) Limited hardware support

Answer: - C

36. Which of the following OS types is most commonly used in spacecraft?

A) Distributed Operating System

B) Batch Operating System

C) RealTime Operating System

D) TimeSharing Operating System

Answer: - C

37. What is the primary purpose of Interprocess Communication (IPC)?

A) Allocating memory to processes

B) Enabling communication between processes

C) Scheduling tasks in the CPU

D) Optimizing virtual memory usage

Answer: - B

38. How does an OS manage file systems?

A) By physically organizing files on storage media

B) By providing a logical structure for storing and retrieving data

C) By running batch processes

D) By clearing memory after file access

Answer: - B

39. Which component of the OS translates user commands into machinereadable instructions?

A) Kernel

B) File System

C) Shell

D) Scheduler

Answer: - C

40. Which OS is most commonly used in smartphones?

A) UNIX

B) Android

C) MSDOS

D) VxWorks

Answer: - B

41. In which OS type are resources shared over a network?

A) Batch Operating System

B) Distributed Operating System

C) RealTime Operating System

D) TimeSharing Operating System

Answer: - B

42. What is the role of a commandline interface (CLI) in an OS?

A) Provides a graphical interface for users

B) Allows users to interact with the OS through text commands

C) Optimizes system resources automatically

D) Updates the OS without user input

Answer: - B

43. Which of the following is a responsibility of I/O management?

A) Managing CPU time

B) Handling communication with external devices

C) Allocating memory to processes

D) Scheduling tasks in realtime

Answer: - B

44. How does the OS handle deadlocks between processes?

A) By terminating all processes

B) By managing resource allocation efficiently

C) By delaying all processes indefinitely

D) By reducing CPU usage

Answer: - B

45. Which operating system is opensource and widely used for servers?

A) Windows

B) Linux

C) macOS

D) VxWorks

Answer: - B

46. What is the role of caching in I/O management?

A) Prevents memory overflows

B) Temporarily stores frequently accessed data to improve speed

C) Clears unnecessary files

D) Restricts unauthorized access

Answer: - B

47. Which OS provides a predictable response time, critical in medical devices?

A) Distributed OS

B) RealTime OS

C) Batch OS

D) TimeSharing OS

Answer: - B

48. Which OS is commonly used in personal computers for userfriendly operation?

A) UNIX

B) MSDOS

C) Windows

D) VxWorks

Answer: - C

49. What is the role of the bootloader in an OS?

A) Handles multiuser requests

B) Loads the OS into memory during startup

C) Manages memory allocation

D) Runs applications directly from storage

Answer: - B

50. What does "fault tolerance" in distributed systems ensure?

A) Immediate task execution

B) System continues functioning even when a part fails

C) Reduced resource sharing

D) Limited multiuser capability

Answer: - B

51. Which of the following is NOT a function of the OS?

A) Process management

B) Memory management

C) Internet browsing

D) I/O management

Answer: - C

52. What type of OS allows multiple users to access a system simultaneously?

A) Distributed Operating System

B) TimeSharing Operating System

C) Batch Operating System

D) RealTime Operating System

Answer: - B

53. Which OS type is known for operating over several connected systems?

A) RealTime Operating System

B) TimeSharing Operating System

C) Distributed Operating System

D) Batch Operating System

Answer: - C

54. What is a key feature of a real-time operating system (RTOS)?

A) High user friendliness

B) Efficient handling of multiple users

C) Predictable and timely task execution

D) Support for running large applications

Answer: - C

55. In process management, what does scheduling refer to?

A) Assigning CPU time to processes

B) Assigning memory to processes

C) Managing the storage devices

D) Allowing users to control process execution

Answer: - A

56. Which of the following is true about timesharing operating systems?

A) They handle single user systems efficiently.

B) Each user gets a fair share of the CPU time.

C) They process jobs in batches.

D) They are only suitable for offline tasks.

Answer: - B

57. Which of the following is a feature of virtual memory?

A) Reduces the need for physical RAM

B) Provides faster CPU processing

C) Ensures each process has exclusive access to RAM

D) Optimizes I/O operations

Answer: - A

58. What is a significant benefit of a distributed operating system?

A) Provides better security than a local OS

B) Allows centralized management of resources

C) Handles processes and resources on a single machine

D) Improves overall system reliability and scalability

Answer: - D

59. Which OS is known for handling processes in a strict, time-dependent order?

A) TimeSharing Operating System

B) RealTime Operating System

C) Batch Operating System

D) Distributed Operating System

Answer: - B

60. In an OS, which component is responsible for managing access to the hardware and providing system services?

A) Shell

B) Kernel

C) Process Scheduler

D) File System

Answer: - B

61. How does an OS ensure that each process runs without interfering with others?

A) Through memory protection

B) By using a virtual machine

C) By allocating resources equally

D) By using timesharing techniques

Answer: - A

62. Which of the following is NOT typically managed by the OS?

A) Network protocols

B) CPU time allocation

C) File storage and retrieval

D) Program code debugging

Answer: - D

63. Which of the following is a characteristic of batch processing?

A) No immediate user interaction

B) Tasks are executed in real time

C) Tasks are performed simultaneously

D) Resources are shared interactively

Answer: - A

64. Which type of operating system allows multiple processes to be executed at the same time by switching between them rapidly?

A) Batch Operating System

B) TimeSharing Operating System

C) Distributed Operating System

D) RealTime Operating System

Answer: - B

65. Which of the following OS types is most likely to be used in a cloud computing environment?

A) RealTime Operating System

B) Batch Operating System

C) Distributed Operating System

D) Embedded Operating System

Answer: - C

66. What does memory protection ensure in an OS?

A) Multiple processes can share the same memory without issues

B) One process cannot overwrite another process's memory

C) The memory is never used by more than one process at a time

D) It allocates extra RAM during system downtime

Answer: - B

67. In a timesharing system, what determines how long a user can interact with the system before switching?

A) The process priority

B) The time slice allocated to the user

C) The amount of memory needed

D) The user's privilege level

Answer: - B

68. What type of OS is typically used in devices such as refrigerators, washing machines, and microwaves?

A) RealTime Operating System

B) Batch Operating System

C) TimeSharing Operating System

D) Distributed Operating System

Answer: - A

69. Which of the following is an example of a distributed OS?

A) Windows

B) UNIX

C) Google's server system

D) macOS

Answer: - C

70. What is the main task of I/O management in an OS?

A) Optimizing memory allocation

B) Facilitating communication between external devices and the OS

C) Managing multiuser operations

D) Ensuring processes don't interfere with each other

Answer: - B

71. Which of the following is a function of the OS kernel?

A) Provide a user interface

B) Manage system memory and resources

C) Execute application programs

D) Translate commands into machine language

Answer: - B

72. Which type of OS is used for real-time decision making, such as in medical equipment?

A) Batch Operating System

B) RealTime Operating System

C) TimeSharing Operating System

D) Distributed Operating System

Answer: - B

73. What is the main difference between a distributed OS and a timesharing OS?

A) Distributed OS shares resources across multiple systems; timesharing OS focuses on single machine efficiency.

B) Timesharing OS operates in real time, while distributed OS processes jobs sequentially.

C) Distributed OS is used by multiple users, while timesharing OS operates in offline environments.

D) Timesharing OS only works on mainframes, while distributed OS is used in embedded systems.

Answer: - A

74. Which feature in an OS allows a program to run even when the physical memory is full?

A) Memory protection

B) Virtual memory

C) Task scheduling

D) CPU prioritization

Answer: - B

75. Which of the following is a primary benefit of using a timesharing system?

A) Allows multiple processes to execute simultaneously

B) Ensures processes execute in real time

C) Provides efficient allocation of CPU time for multiple users

D) Optimizes memory usage for large applications

Answer: - C

76. How does the OS improve the user experience in graphical user interfaces (GUIs)?

A) By providing a command line interface

B) By using text based commands

C) By offering visual elements like windows and icons

D) By limiting user control over system processes

Answer: - C

77. In which type of operating system do multiple users use a single system at the same time, such as in university mainframe systems?

A) Batch Operating System

B) TimeSharing Operating System

C) Distributed Operating System

D) RealTime Operating System

Answer: - B

78. Which is a key benefit of virtual memory?

A) Allows running programs larger than the physical memory

B) Prevents I/O errors

C) Enhances user interaction

D) Increases CPU speed

Answer: - A

79. In an OS, what does the process scheduler manage?

A) The allocation of memory

B) The allocation of CPU time to various tasks

C) Communication between processes

D) External devices like printers and monitors

Answer: - B

80. Which of the following is an example of a batch processing system?

A) UNIX

B) MSDOS

C) Payroll processing system

D) Google's cloud infrastructure

Answer: - C

81. Which of the following is a key role of the OS kernel?

A) Provide security updates

B) Manage hardware resources

C) Facilitate user interactions

D) Run applications

Answer: - B

82. Which type of operating system is used in systems requiring precise timing and quick responses to external events?

A) Distributed Operating System

B) Batch Operating System

C) RealTime Operating System

D) TimeSharing Operating System

Answer: - C

83. What is an example of a device that typically uses a RealTime Operating System?

A) Desktop computer

B) Smartphone

C) Medical devices like pacemakers

D) Web servers

Answer: - C

84. What does an OS do to prevent a process from accessing the memory of another process?

A) Resource Allocation

B) Virtual Memory

C) Memory Protection

D) Process Scheduling

Answer: - C

85. Which OS is often used in academic and research environments where many users need to access a system simultaneously?

A) UNIX

B) macOS

C) Windows

D) RealTime Operating System

Answer: - A

86. What is the main advantage of multitasking in an operating system?

A) It allows the CPU to process only one task at a time.

B) It ensures applications can run efficiently by utilizing CPU time effectively.

C) It reduces the need for memory allocation.

D) It limits the number of processes that can run.

Answer: - B

87. What type of operating system is designed to control specialized devices like automobiles or microwave ovens?

A) RealTime Operating System

B) Distributed Operating System

C) TimeSharing Operating System

D) Batch Operating System

Answer: - A

88. What is a time slice in a timesharing system?

A) The time allocated to a process to complete its execution

B) The amount of memory assigned to a user's task

C) The total execution time of a program

D) The interval between data transfers to and from external devices

Answer: - A

89. What is the primary function of an I/O device driver?

A) Manage memory allocation for I/O operations

B) Allow the OS to communicate with external hardware devices

C) Prevent processes from interfering with I/O operations

D) Schedule I/O tasks based on priority

Answer: - B

90. Which type of OS is best suited for handling complex, time sensitive tasks, such as controlling robotic systems in manufacturing?

A) TimeSharing Operating System

B) Distributed Operating System

C) RealTime Operating System

D) Batch Operating System

Answer: - C

91. What is the primary benefit of using a distributed operating system in a networked environment?

A) It improves security by separating system processes.

B) It allows for the management of multiple devices on a single network.

C) It consolidates computing resources for improved performance and scalability.

D) It reduces the cost of managing a single system.

Answer: - C

92. What is the key difference between a process and a program in an OS context?

A) A process is a running instance of a program, while a program is static and not executing.

B) A program is an executed process, while a process is a system application.

C) A process does not use system resources, but a program does.

D) There is no difference; the terms are interchangeable.

Answer: - A

93. What is a major characteristic of an embedded operating system?

A) It allows multiuser support.

B) It runs on a network of servers.

C) It is optimized for hardware with limited resources.

D) It provides extensive software updates.

Answer: - C

94. Which of the following is NOT typically managed by the OS's process scheduler?

A) CPU allocation

B) Task priority

C) Process execution time

D) Memory allocation

Answer: - D

95. What is an example of an operating system used for embedded systems?

A) Windows Server

B) Android

C) VxWorks

D) macOS

Answer: - C

96. How does a distributed operating system improve fault tolerance?

A) By ensuring that one system can take over tasks if another system fails

B) By reducing the need for system updates

C) By preventing the network from experiencing failures

D) By restricting access to only certain users

Answer: - A

97. In which of the following scenarios would a batch operating system be most beneficial?

A) Running interactive video games

B) Performing largescale data processing tasks

C) Providing real-time responses to user input

D) Managing cloud-based computing resources

Answer: - B

98. What is one of the primary advantages of a virtual memory system?

A) It makes more physical memory available than is actually installed in the computer.

B) It increases the speed of the processor.

C) It reduces the complexity of managing multiple users.

D) It prevents processes from sharing data.

Answer: - A

99. Which of the following is true about memory management in an OS?

A) The OS allocates memory to processes as needed and deallocates it when processes terminate.

B) Memory management is not necessary in modern operating systems.

C) The OS prevents any process from using virtual memory.

D) All processes share the same block of memory for efficiency.

Answer: - A

100. Which of the following OS types is typically used for systems with a single user or limited user access?

A) RealTime Operating System

B) TimeSharing Operating System

C) Distributed Operating System

D) Batch Operating System

Answer: - D

"Networking Fundamentals" : -

1. What is the primary purpose of networking?
A) To store files on a server

B) To connect multiple devices for data sharing and communication
C) To secure a computer's data
D) To manage the internet connection
Answer: - B

2. Which of the following is an example of a Local Area Network (LAN)?
A) The internet
B) A network connecting devices in an office building
C) A global communication network
D) A citywide network
Answer: - B

3. What does WAN stand for?
A) Wireless Area Network
B) Wide Area Network
C) Web Area Network
D) World Area Network
Answer: - B

4. What is the defining characteristic of a Metropolitan Area Network (MAN)?
A) Covers a city or large campus
B) Connects devices within a small area
C) Can span continents
D) Uses wireless technology only
Answer: - A

5. Which of the following is an example of a Wide Area Network (WAN)?
A) A local office network

B) A network connecting multiple cities or countries
C) A network within a home
D) A private network inside a building
Answer: - B

6. What protocol is primarily used for communication over the internet?
A) TCP/IP
B) UDP
C) FTP
D) SMTP
Answer: - A

7. Which layer of the OSI model is responsible for routing data packets?
A) Physical Layer
B) Data Link Layer

C) Network Layer

D) Transport Layer

Answer: - C

8. Which OSI model layer handles error detection and correction in data transmission?

A) Application Layer

B) Presentation Layer

C) Data Link Layer

D) Network Layer

Answer: - C

9. Which OSI layer is closest to the user and provides network services like email and web browsing?

A) Physical Layer

B) Data Link Layer

C) Transport Layer

D) Application Layer

Answer: - D

10. What is the role of the Transport Layer in the OSI model?

A) Ensures reliable data transfer and handles flow control

B) Defines the physical medium for transmission

C) Routes data packets to their destination

D) Formats and encrypts data for transmission

Answer: - A

11. Which IP address type uses a 32bit address format?

A) IPv4

B) IPv6

C) Domain Name System

D) MAC Address

Answer: - A

12. Which of the following is an example of a domain name?

A) 192.168.1.1

B) google.com

C) 255.255.255.0

D) 3001: -0db8: -85a3: -0000: -0000: -8a2e: -0370: -7334

Answer: - B

13. What is the function of the Domain Name System (DNS)?

A) To assign IP addresses to devices

B) To convert domain names into IP addresses

C) To create network security protocols

D) To manage email services

Answer: - B

14. What type of network is typically used to connect computers in a single office or home?

A) MAN

B) LAN

C) WAN

D) Internet

Answer: - B

15. Which of the following is NOT a characteristic of a Wide Area Network (WAN)?

A) It connects devices over long distances

B) It uses highspeed internet for communication

C) It typically covers a small area like a home or office

D) It can span across cities or countries

Answer: - C

16. Which of the following layers in the OSI model is responsible for the actual transmission of raw bits over the physical medium?

A) Application Layer

B) Physical Layer

C) Transport Layer

D) Network Layer

Answer: - B

17. In which layer of the OSI model is data compression and encryption handled?

A) Data Link Layer

B) Application Layer

C) Presentation Layer

D) Network Layer

Answer: - C

18. What is the role of the Session Layer in the OSI model?

A) Ensures data integrity

B) Manages sessions or connections between devices

C) Defines how data should be formatted for transmission

D) Provides routing for data packets

Answer: - B

19. Which layer of the OSI model is responsible for ensuring reliable data transfer?

A) Transport Layer

B) Network Layer

C) Physical Layer

D) Application Layer

Answer: - A

20. What does IP stand for in IP address?

A) Internet Protocol

B) Internet Provision

C) Internal Protocol

D) Information Pathway

Answer: - A

21. Which of the following IP address formats allows for a larger pool of addresses?

A) IPv4

B) IPv5

C) IPv6

D) IPv3

Answer: - C

22. Which protocol is used to send emails?

A) TCP

B) HTTP

C) SMTP

D) FTP

Answer: - C

23. Which type of network would be most suitable for connecting devices within a city?

A) LAN

B) WAN

C) MAN

D) Internet

Answer: - C

24. Which layer in the OSI model would a router operate at?

A) Network Layer

B) Data Link Layer

C) Transport Layer

D) Application Layer

Answer: - A

25. Which of the following is an example of Platform as a Service (PaaS)?

A) Google Drive

B) Amazon Web Services

C) Google App Engine

D) Dropbox

Answer: - C

26. Which of the following is NOT a feature of cloud computing?

A) On-demand access to resources

B) Cost efficiency through hardware sharing

C) Local installation of all software

D) Scalability based on user needs

Answer: - C

27. Which of the following is an example of Software as a Service (SaaS)?

A) Microsoft Office 365

B) Amazon EC2

C) Google Compute Engine

D) Dropbox

Answer: - A

28. What is the purpose of a Local Area Network (LAN)?

A) To connect devices across multiple cities

B) To connect devices over a vast geographic area

C) To connect devices within a small area like a home or office

D) To provide wireless internet connections

Answer: - C

29. What does cloud computing primarily provide?

A) Hardware storage only

B) On-demand computing services over the internet

C) Data security and encryption

D) Local data backups

Answer: - B

30. What is an IPv4 address?

A) 128bit address

B) 32bit address

C) 64bit address

D) 256bit address

Answer: - B

31. Which of the following is NOT part of the OSI model?

A) Physical Layer

B) Application Layer

C) Transmission Layer

D) Network Layer

Answer: - C

32. What is the main purpose of the Transport Layer in the OSI model?

A) Routing data packets to the correct destination

B) Ensuring data is correctly formatted and readable

C) Ensuring reliable data transfer between devices

D) Encoding and compressing data for transmission

Answer: - C

33. What type of network is used to connect devices within a building?

A) WAN

B) MAN

C) LAN

D) Internet

Answer: - C

34. What is a common use of a Wide Area Network (WAN)?

A) Connecting devices within a small office

B) Connecting multiple cities or countries over long distances

C) Connecting devices on a local campus

D) Connecting personal devices in a home

Answer: - B

35. What does the Application Layer in the OSI model do?

A) Manages communication between devices

B) Ensures errorfree data transmission

C) Provides network services to the user

D) Encrypts and formats the data

Answer: - C

36. What is an IP address used for?

A) Encrypting network traffic

B) Identifying devices on a network

C) Defining network protocols

D) Compressing data during transmission

Answer: - B

37. Which layer of the OSI model is responsible for error detection and correction in transmitted data?

A) Application Layer

B) Data Link Layer

C) Network Layer

D) Transport Layer

Answer: - B

38. What does DNS stand for?

A) Domain Naming System

B) Data Network Service

C) Domain Name System

D) Digital Network Service

Answer: - C

39. Which type of cloud computing service provides infrastructure like virtual machines and storage?

A) SaaS

B) IaaS

C) PaaS

D) DaaS

Answer: - B

40. What is the main function of the Physical Layer in the OSI model?

A) Transmitting raw bits over the physical medium

B) Formatting data for the receiving application

C) Ensuring reliable data transfer between devices

D) Routing data packets through the network

Answer: - A

41. Which of the following is an example of a Metropolitan Area Network (MAN)?

A) A home Wi-Fi network

B) A network spanning a city to connect schools and businesses

C) A global network like the internet

D) A small office network

Answer: - B

42. Which of the following protocols is used to send data over the web?

A) SMTP

B) TCP

C) HTTP

D) FTP

Answer: - C

43. In which of the following layers of the OSI model does encryption of data occur?

A) Network Layer

B) Presentation Layer

C) Data Link Layer

D) Transport Layer

Answer: - B

44. What does the Session Layer in the OSI model do?

A) Ensures secure data transmission

B) Manages sessions between applications

C) Routes data packets between devices

D) Encrypts and compresses data

Answer: - B

45. What is the main difference between IPv4 and IPv6 addresses?

A) IPv4 uses 128bit addresses while IPv6 uses 32bit

B) IPv4 uses 32bit addresses while IPv6 uses 128bit

C) IPv4 is used for local networks, while IPv6 is for global networks

D) IPv6 has no address limitations

Answer: - B

46. Which type of network is used to connect devices over a large area, often across countries or continents?

A) LAN

B) MAN

C) WAN

D) Internet

Answer: - C

47. What does cloud computing allow users to do?

A) Access computing resources over the internet

B) Store data only on local hard drives

C) Use only physical servers for applications

D) Prevent the use of virtual machines

Answer: - A

48. What type of cloud computing service allows users to develop applications without managing underlying infrastructure?

A) IaaS

B) PaaS

C) SaaS

D) DaaS

Answer: - B

49. What is the purpose of a Domain Name System (DNS)?

A) To assign IP addresses to devices

B) To translate domain names into IP addresses

C) To define the structure of a network

D) To manage security for a network

Answer: - B

50. What type of cloud computing service provides software applications via the internet?

A) IaaS

B) PaaS

C) SaaS

D) DaaS

Answer: - C

51. What does WAN stand for?

A) Wireless Area Network

B) Web Access Network

C) Wide Area Network

D) World Area Network

Answer: - C

52. Which of the following is a characteristic of a Local Area Network (LAN)?

A) Covers a wide geographical area

B) Has high latency and low bandwidth

C) Connects devices in a small area, like an office

D) Only uses wireless devices

Answer: - C

53. Which layer of the OSI model is responsible for routing data to the correct destination?

A) Network Layer

B) Data Link Layer

C) Transport Layer

D) Physical Layer

Answer: - A

54. What is the purpose of the Data Link Layer in the OSI model?

A) Formatting data for the application layer

B) Ensuring data is errorfree during transmission

C) Managing sessions between devices

D) Routing data packets through the network

Answer: - B

55. What does the Transport Layer in the OSI model handle?

A) Ensuring reliable data transfer

B) Encoding data for transmission

C) Defining the physical medium for data transmission

D) Routing packets to their destination

Answer: - A

56. Which layer of the OSI model defines how data should be formatted for transmission?

A) Application Layer

B) Data Link Layer

C) Network Layer

D) Presentation Layer

Answer: - D

57. What is the purpose of the Physical Layer in the OSI model?

A) Defining the physical connections and transmission medium

B) Ensuring data integrity and error correction

C) Providing services to the application layer

D) Managing the logical addressing of devices

Answer: - A

58. What does an IP address do in a network?

A) It identifies the location of a device on a network

B) It provides security for transmitted data

C) It defines the routing protocols for data transfer

D) It converts domain names into readable formats

Answer: - A

59. Which of the following is an example of Software as a Service (SaaS)?

A) Amazon Web Services

B) Microsoft Office 365

C) Google App Engine

D) Microsoft Azure

Answer: - B

60. Which type of network is most suitable for connecting devices across a large city?

A) LAN

B) WAN

C) MAN

D) Internet

Answer: - C

61. What is the main role of the Network Layer in the OSI model?

A) To route data packets to the correct destination

B) To encrypt data for secure transmission

C) To split large data packets into smaller ones

D) To manage communication sessions between devices

Answer: - A

62. Which of the following is an example of a physical connection in the Physical Layer?

A) Ethernet cable

B) IP address

C) Data packet

D) MAC address

Answer: - A

63. What is the purpose of the Session Layer in the OSI model?

A) Ensures data is correctly formatted and readable

B) Manages sessions or connections between devices

C) Routes data packets to their destination

D) Transmits raw bits over a physical medium

Answer: - B

64. What does IPv6 offer that IPv4 does not?

A) A 128bit address space

B) A 32bit address space

C) Faster data transmission

D) A smaller address pool

Answer: - A

65. What is the main difference between a LAN and a WAN?

A) LAN covers a larger geographical area than WAN

B) WAN uses wireless communication while LAN uses wired

C) WAN connects devices over longer distances compared to LAN

D) LAN connects devices globally while WAN connects devices locally

Answer: - C

66. Which type of cloud service allows users to access virtualized computing resources like servers and storage?

A) SaaS

B) IaaS

C) PaaS

D) DaaS

Answer: - B

67. What does the Application Layer in the OSI model support?

A) Basic data transmission

B) Secure data transfer

C) User level interactions and services like email and web browsing

D) Error detection and correction

Answer: - C

68. What is the main feature of a Wide Area Network (WAN)?

A) High speed and low latency

B) Coverage of small areas like homes and offices

C) Coverage over large geographical areas, such as countries or continents

D) Exclusive use of wireless technology

Answer: - C

69. What is a characteristic of the Presentation Layer in the OSI model?

A) It manages the transmission of raw data

B) It formats and encrypts data for transmission

C) It ensures data integrity during transfer

D) It controls the flow of data across a network

Answer: - B

70. What is the role of a router in a network?

A) To direct traffic between different networks

B) To manage local area connections

C) To encrypt data packets

D) To monitor the physical layer of a network

Answer: - A

71. Which of the following cloud services is best suited for application development?

A) SaaS

B) IaaS

C) PaaS

D) DaaS

Answer: - C

72. Which of the following protocols is used to securely send emails?

A) SMTP

B) POP3

C) IMAP

D) HTTPS

Answer: - A

73. Which layer of the OSI model deals with error correction and retransmission of lost packets?

A) Application Layer

B) Transport Layer

C) Network Layer

D) Data Link Layer

Answer: - B

74. What is a primary function of the Data Link Layer in networking?

A) Defining IP addresses

B) Routing data packets

C) Providing errorfree data transfer

D) Encrypting data for secure transmission

Answer: - C

75. What is the primary function of the OSI model's Physical Layer?

A) Encrypt data packets

B) Format data for network transmission

C) Manage the flow of data between devices

D) Define the physical medium for data transmission

Answer: - D

76. What does the acronym DNS stand for?

A) Digital Network Service

B) Domain Name Service

C) Domain Name System

D) Data Network System

Answer: - C

77. What is an example of a service that uses the SaaS model?

A) Dropbox

B) Google Drive

C) Microsoft Office 365

D) Amazon EC2

Answer: - C

78. Which of the following is NOT a function of the Network Layer in the OSI model?

A) Routing data packets

B) Defining logical addressing

C) Establishing sessions between devices

D) Providing reliable communication

Answer: - C

79. Which of the following is true about IPv4?

A) It uses 128bit addresses

B) It provides a larger address space than IPv6

C) It is being replaced by IPv6

D) It supports unlimited devices

Answer: - C

80. Which type of cloud service allows users to run applications without needing to manage the underlying infrastructure?

A) PaaS

B) IaaS

C) SaaS

D) DaaS

Answer: - A

81. Which of the following is an example of a LAN?

A) The internet

B) A network connecting all devices within a small office

C) A network connecting multiple cities

D) A network connecting devices in a public park

Answer: - B

82. In which layer of the OSI model does a router operate?

A) Network Layer

B) Transport Layer

C) Data Link Layer

D) Application Layer

Answer: - A

83. What is the main function of the Transport Layer?

A) Routing data between devices

B) Providing errorfree data transmission

C) Splitting data into smaller packets and reassembling them

D) Defining the physical medium for data transmission

Answer: - C

84. What does the Presentation Layer of the OSI model primarily do?

A) Routes data packets to the correct destination

B) Translates data between different formats and encrypts it

C) Handles error detection during transmission

D) Ensures reliable transmission of data across the network

Answer: - B

85. What type of network covers an entire city?

A) LAN

B) WAN

C) MAN

D) Internet

Answer: - C

86. What is the role of the Application Layer in networking?

A) It handles the physical connection between devices

B) It supports user applications such as browsers and email

C) It ensures errorfree transmission of data

D) It routes data packets to the correct destination

Answer: - B

87. Which of the following is true about cloud computing?

A) It requires the use of local storage only

B) It is only available to large enterprises

C) It allows users to access computing resources over the internet

D) It is primarily used for data encryption

Answer: - C

88. What is the purpose of an IP address?

A) To secure data during transmission

B) To identify and locate devices on a network

C) To define the session parameters between two devices

D) To format data for application use

Answer: - B

89. Which of the following cloud services provides a platform for building and hosting applications?

A) IaaS

B) SaaS

C) PaaS

D) DaaS

Answer: - C

90. What is a WAN typically used for?

A) Connecting devices within a single building

B) Connecting devices across a country or globally

C) Sharing resources within a small office

D) Managing local network traffic

Answer: - B

Primary vs. Secondary Storage

1. What is the primary characteristic of primary storage?

A) Non-volatile

B) Stores data temporarily

C) Used for long term storage

D) Slower than secondary storage

Answer: - B

2. Which of the following is a type of primary storage?

A) Hard Disk Drive

B) Solid State Drive

C) Random Access Memory

D) Cloud Storage

Answer: - C

3. What happens to the data in RAM when the computer is turned off?

A) It is saved automatically

B) It is transferred to secondary storage

C) It is lost

D) It is encrypted

Answer: - C

4. What is the purpose of Read Only Memory (ROM)?

A) Store frequently accessed files

B) Store critical system information

C) Temporarily store data being processed

D) Enhance overall performance

Answer: - B

5. Which of the following is a non-volatile memory type?

A) RAM

B) ROM

C) Cache memory

D) Registers

Answer: - B

6. What type of data is typically stored in ROM?

A) User files

B) Running applications

C) Computer firmware

D) Temporary system files

Answer: - C

7. Which of these is an example of secondary storage?

A) ROM

B) Cache

C) SSD

D) Registers

Answer: - C

8. What is a key advantage of SSDs over HDDs?

A) Larger storage capacity

B) Lower cost per GB

C) Faster data access speeds

D) More moving parts

Answer: - C

9. What does a Hard Disk Drive use to store data?

A) Flash memory

B) Magnetic disks

C) Optical media

D) Electric currents

Answer: - B

10. Which storage device has no moving parts?

A) HDD

B) SSD

C) Floppy Disk

D) Tape Drive

Answer: - B

11. What is a database?

A) A system for managing files

B) A structured collection of data

C) A physical storage device

D) A type of memory

Answer: - B

12. Which database component stores data in rows and columns?

A) Field

B) Record

C) Table

D) Schema

Answer: - C

13. What is a record in a database?

A) A single row in a table

B) A column of data

C) A table relationship

D) A database file

Answer: - A

14. In database terminology, what is a field?

A) A row in a table

B) A single data point in a record

C) A collection of tables

D) A database schema

Answer: - B

15. What is a key advantage of using a database over flat file storage?

A) Better organization and accessibility

B) Higher data redundancy

C) Simpler structure

D) No need for security measures

Answer: - A

16. Which type of database uses tables to store data?

A) NoSQL

B) Relational

C) Document based

D) Key value

Answer: - B

17. What connects tables in a relational database?

A) Indexes

B) Keys

C) Graphs

D) Arrays

Answer: - B

18. Which database type is best for handling unstructured data?

A) Relational

B) NoSQL

C) SQL

D) Hierarchical

Answer: - B

19. What is an example of a relational database system?

A) MongoDB

B) Redis

C) MySQL

D) Cassandra

Answer: - C

20. Which database type is ideal for big data applications?

A) Relational

B) NoSQL

C) Flat file

D) Object oriented

Answer: - B

21. What is the 321 backup rule?

A) 3 backups, 2 onsite, 1 cloud-based

B) 3 copies, 2 formats, 1 offsite

C) 3 backups, 2 in the cloud, 1 physical copy

D) 3 types of storage, 2 automatic backups, 1 manual backup

Answer: - B

22. Which of the following is a cloud storage service?

A) BIOS

B) Google Drive

C) RAM

D) SSD

Answer: - B

23. Why is encryption important for data?

A) It increases storage capacity

B) It improves backup speeds

C) It prevents unauthorized access

D) It eliminates redundancy

Answer: - C

24. What is the purpose of automating backups?

A) To reduce storage costs

B) To eliminate manual backup efforts

C) To improve database performance

D) To secure the primary storage

Answer: - B

25. Which tool alerts users to potential hard drive failures?

A) BIOS

B) Health monitoring software

C) ROM

D) Cloud storage

Answer: - B

26. What type of storage is best for long term data preservation?

A) RAM

B) ROM

C) Secondary storage

D) Cache memory

Answer: - C

27. Which of the following is the fastest type of memory?

A) RAM

B) SSD

C) Cache memory

D) HDD

Answer: - C

28. Which storage type is commonly used for the operating system?

A) RAM

B) ROM

C) HDD or SSD

D) Flash Drive

Answer: - C

29. What is the primary disadvantage of HDDs compared to SSDs?

A) Higher cost

B) Smaller capacity

C) Slower read/write speeds

D) Less durability

Answer: - C

30. What makes SSDs more durable than HDDs?

A) Higher storage capacity

B) No moving parts

C) Better encryption methods

D) Faster data transfer

Answer: - B

31. What is a primary key in a database?

A) A unique identifier for a record

B) A column that stores encrypted data

C) A key used to encrypt database files

D) A table's default sorting order

Answer: - A

32. Which field type allows storing large text or paragraphs in a database?

A) Integer

B) Boolean

C) Text

D) Decimal

Answer: - C

33. What is a foreign key?

A) A column used for indexing

B) A column that connects two tables

C) A unique identifier for a table

D) A key for encrypting data

Answer: - B

34. What is the role of indexes in a database?

A) Encrypt the database

B) Improve query performance

C) Backup data

D) Remove redundant data

Answer: - B

35. What is the term for duplicating the same data in multiple locations in a database?

A) Indexing

B) Normalization

C) Redundancy

D) Encryption

Answer: - C

36. Which database structure is best for hierarchical data representation?

A) Relational

B) NoSQL

C) Graph

D) Hierarchical

Answer: - D

37. Which NoSQL database type uses key value pairs?

A) Document based

B) Key value

C) Relational

D) Columnar

Answer: - B

38. What is the main benefit of NoSQL databases?

A) Higher speed for structured data

B) Handling unstructured data efficiently

C) Simplified SQL queries

D) Enhanced table relationships

Answer: - B

39. Which database is used for analyzing large datasets in real time?

A) PostgreSQL

B) MySQL

C) Cassandra

D) Access

Answer: - C

40. What type of data is stored in document based NoSQL databases?

A) Structured

B) Binary

C) Unstructured or semi structured

D) Encrypted

Answer: - C

41. Why is cloud storage beneficial?

A) Faster than RAM

B) Increases physical storage

C) Provides remote access and redundancy

D) Eliminates the need for SSDs

Answer: - C

42. What is one disadvantage of cloud storage?

A) Slow speeds

B) Limited accessibility

C) Potential data security risks

D) High hardware costs

Answer: - C

43. How does disk cleanup improve system performance?

A) Increases storage capacity

B) Removes unnecessary files

C) Optimizes database queries

D) Reduces encryption time

Answer: - B

44. What type of data should always be encrypted?

A) Media files

B) Personal or sensitive information

C) System logs

D) Temporary files

Answer: - B

45. Why is monitoring storage health important?

A) To reduce storage costs

B) To detect potential hardware failures early

C) To optimize database schema

D) To prevent data duplication

Answer: - B

46. What is a NAS device used for?

A) Highspeed computation

B) Network attached storage for backups

C) Realtime data analysis

D) Cloud computing

Answer: - B

47. How does regular data organization help users?

A) Reduces system crashes

B) Prevents unauthorized access

C) Ensures easy retrieval and efficiency

D) Increases database size

Answer: - C

48. What does "redundancy" in backup strategies mean?

A) Extra copies of data stored in multiple locations

B) Removing duplicate files

C) Automatically archiving old data

D) Compressing large files

Answer: - A

49. Why should backup data be stored offsite?

A) To reduce local storage usage

B) To ensure data safety in case of local disasters

C) To prevent accidental deletion

D) To encrypt the data better

Answer: - B

50. Which of the following is an example of automated backup software?

A) BIOS

B) Time Machine

C) RAM Optimizer

D) Data Cleanup Tool

Answer: - B

51. What is the 321 backup rule?

A) 3 copies of data, 2 stored on the same device, 1 in the cloud

B) 3 copies of data, 2 formats, 1 offsite

C) 3 backups per day, 2 stored locally, 1 archived monthly

D) 3 devices, 2 users, 1 backup

Answer: - B

52. Which tool is commonly used for cloud based file storage and sharing?

A) SQLite

B) OneDrive

C) BIOS

D) Disk Defragmenter

Answer: - B

53. How does encryption protect sensitive data?

A) By creating backups automatically

B) By converting data into a secure code

C) By splitting data into smaller packets

D) By organizing files into folders

Answer: - B

54. Which device is used for local, network based storage in businesses?

A) Cloud storage

B) External HDD

C) NAS (Network Attached Storage)

D) SSD

Answer: - C

55. What is the purpose of a health check tool for storage devices?

A) To remove unnecessary files

B) To encrypt stored data

C) To monitor drive reliability and detect errors

D) To increase storage capacity

Answer: - C

56. Which of the following is volatile memory?

A) SSD

B) HDD

C) RAM

D) Cloud Storage

Answer: - C

57. Why is SSD preferred for modern computing?

A) Lower cost

B) Larger capacity

C) Faster read/write speeds and durability

D) Builtin redundancy

Answer: - C

58. What distinguishes ROM from RAM?

A) ROM is volatile, and RAM is nonvolatile

B) ROM retains data permanently; RAM does not

C) ROM is used for temporary storage; RAM is for permanent storage

D) ROM is faster than RAM

Answer: - B

59. Which storage device typically uses spinning disks?

A) SSD

B) HDD

C) USB Flash Drive

D) RAM

Answer: - B

60. What does the term "nonvolatile" mean in storage?

A) Data is erased after power is off

B) Data remains stored even when power is off

C) Storage has limited lifespan

D) Storage is connected via a network

Answer: - B

61. What does the acronym SQL stand for?

A) Structured Query Logic

B) System Quality Language

C) Structured Query Language

D) System Query Logic

Answer: - C

62. In a relational database, which of the following defines a unique value for a table row?

A) Index

B) Foreign key

C) Primary key

D) Query

Answer: - C

63. Which type of database stores data in rows and columns?

A) Document based database

B) Relational database

C) Graph database

D) Key value database

Answer: - B

64. What is the purpose of normalization in databases?

A) To duplicate data across tables

B) To improve query performance

C) To reduce data redundancy and improve data integrity

D) To encrypt sensitive data

Answer: - C

65. Which NoSQL database is best for handling unstructured data like JSON files?

A) MySQL

B) MongoDB

C) PostgreSQL

D) Oracle

Answer: - B

66. Which database type is ideal for real-time web applications?

A) Relational databases

B) NoSQL databases

C) Hierarchical databases

D) File-based databases

Answer: - B

67. What is a graph database used for?

A) Managing structured data with tables

B) Representing relationships between data

C) Storing multimedia files

D) Performing data backups

Answer: - B

68. Which query language is used with relational databases?

A) XPath

B) SQL

C) JSONPath

D) HiveQL

Answer: - B

69. What is the role of a "foreign key" in a relational database?

A) It ensures data encryption

B) It connects rows in different tables

C) It retrieves records faster

D) It removes data duplicates

Answer: - B

70. Which of the following is an example of a relational database system?

A) Redis

B) MySQL

C) Cassandra

D) Neo4j

Answer: - B

71. What is the primary advantage of automated backups?

A) It reduces file size

B) It ensures regular data backups without manual intervention

C) It organizes files into folders automatically

D) It increases computer speed

Answer: - B

72. Which cloud platform is commonly used for file backups?

A) BIOS

B) Dropbox

C) SQLite

D) PostgreSQL

Answer: - B

73. What does RAID stand for in data storage?

A) Redundant Array of Independent Disks

B) Random Access Indexed Database

C) Recovery and Automated Integration Disk

D) Realtime Access to Independent Data

Answer: - A

74. Which RAID level provides both redundancy and improved performance?

A) RAID 0

B) RAID 1

C) RAID 5

D) RAID 10

Answer: - D

75. What is one downside of local storage compared to cloud storage?

A) Higher speed

B) Limited accessibility from remote locations

C) Increased redundancy

D) Faster backups

Answer: - B

76. Which of the following is NOT a type of cloud service?

A) IaaS

B) PaaS

C) SaaS

D) NAS

Answer: - D

77. How can sensitive data on a storage device be protected before disposal?

A) Deleting files

B) Encrypting the device

C) Formatting the drive

D) Physically destroying the device

Answer: - D

78. What type of backup only saves changes since the last backup?

A) Full backup

B) Incremental backup

C) Differential backup

D) Encrypted backup

Answer: - B

79. Which of the following is NOT an advantage of SSDs over HDDs?

A) Faster performance

B) Higher durability

C) Lower cost per GB

D) Silent operation

Answer: - C

80. What does "scalability" in cloud storage mean?

A) Ability to shrink storage capacity as needed

B) Ability to add or reduce resources based on demand

C) Ability to automate backups

D) Ability to retrieve data faster

Answer: - B

81. What is the primary function of NAS (Network Attached Storage)?

A) Storing data in the cloud

B) Providing shared access to files over a network

C) Encrypting sensitive files

D) Increasing processing speed

Answer: - B

82. Which of the following is an advantage of cloud backups?

A) Completely offline storage

B) Higher speeds than SSDs

C) Remote access to files

D) Requires no internet connection

Answer: - C

83. What is the main disadvantage of using HDDs compared to SSDs?

A) Lower durability and slower performance

B) Higher cost per GB

C) Limited compatibility with modern devices

D) Smaller storage capacity

Answer: - A

84. Which device is best for short term, highspeed data processing?

A) HDD

B) RAM

C) Cloud Storage

D) SSD

Answer: - B

85. What kind of data is typically stored in a document based NoSQL database?

A) Binary files

B) Text and multimedia files

C) JSON, XML, or BSON data

D) Tables with rows and columns

Answer: - C

86. What does "scaling horizontally" mean for databases?

A) Adding more storage to the existing database server

B) Adding more database servers to distribute the load

C) Optimizing the database query performance

D) Decreasing the physical size of the database

Answer: - B

87. Which database type is commonly used for social network relationships?

A) Key value store

B) Graph database

C) Relational database

D) Document database

Answer: - B

88. What is a "query" in the context of databases?

A) A set of rules for data encryption

B) A request to retrieve or manipulate data

C) A backup procedure for database systems

D) A format for unstructured data storage

Answer: - B

89. Which of these is a characteristic of relational databases?

A) Stores data in graphs

B) Uses tables with predefined schema

C) Does not support ACID properties

D) Best suited for storing JSON files

Answer: - B

90. What is ACID compliance in databases?

A) A set of properties ensuring database transactions are reliable

B) A method for organizing files in storage

C) A framework for encrypting sensitive database entries

D) A mechanism to enable automated backups

Answer: - A

91. What is the main feature of differential backups?

A) Backs up only new and changed files since the last full backup

B) Backs up all files regardless of changes

C) Requires no full backup

D) Encrypts data during the backup process

Answer: - A

92. Which of the following is a disadvantage of cloud storage?

A) Limited accessibility

B) High vulnerability to data breaches if not secured

C) No automatic backup features

D) Requires specialized hardware

Answer: - B

93. What is the purpose of RAID 1?

A) Provides no redundancy, only increased performance

B) Mirrors data across multiple drives for redundancy

C) Stripes data across drives without redundancy

D) Combines mirroring and striping

Answer: - B

94. What is the primary risk of not encrypting sensitive data in storage?

A) Loss of data integrity

B) Increased storage costs

C) Unauthorized access to data

D) Slower data retrieval

Answer: - C

95. Which software tool is used for creating and managing relational databases?

A) Google Drive

B) MySQL

C) Redis

D) MongoDB

Answer: - B

96. What happens to data in volatile memory when the power is off?

A) Data is saved automatically

B) Data is lost permanently

C) Data is transferred to secondary storage

D) Data is compressed

Answer: - B

97. What makes SSDs more durable than HDDs?

A) Higher storage capacity

B) No moving parts

C) Compatibility with RAID configurations

D) Increased encryption capabilities

Answer: - B

98. What is the advantage of using an incremental backup over a full backup?

A) Easier restoration process

B) Requires less time and storage space

C) No need for previous backup files

D) Ensures data is always encrypted

Answer: - B

99. Which type of database would best handle time series data?

A) Document database

B) Graph database

C) Key value store

D) Timeseries database (e.g., InfluxDB)

Answer: - D

100. What does it mean when a backup is "redundant"?

A) The backup is stored in multiple locations

B) The backup replaces the original data

C) The backup is encrypted

D) The backup is compressed

Answer: - A

Cybersecurity : -

1. What is the primary goal of cybersecurity?

A) Improve computer performance

B) Protect data, systems, and networks from attacks

C) Increase internet speed

D) Enable remote access to devices

Answer: - B

2. Which of the following is NOT a reason why cybersecurity is important?

A) Protection of personal information

B) Prevention of financial loss

C) Enhancing gaming performance

D) Safeguarding critical infrastructure

Answer: - C

3. How does cybersecurity contribute to national security?

A) By preventing natural disasters

B) By protecting government systems and critical infrastructure

C) By providing financial assistance to citizens

D) By blocking access to social media platforms

Answer: - B

4. What role does cybersecurity play in maintaining trust?

A) It simplifies online transactions

B) It ensures user data remains secure

C) It reduces the need for strong passwords

D) It automates system updates

Answer: - B

5. What could happen if critical infrastructure is targeted by a cyberattack?

A) Increased system efficiency

B) Widespread disruptions to essential services

C) Faster internet connectivity

D) Improved cybersecurity measures

Answer: - B

6. What is a computer virus?

A) A type of antivirus software

B) A malicious program that attaches itself to legitimate files

C) A hardware failure in a computer system

D) A tool used for secure data transfer

Answer: - B

7. What is malware?

A) A type of security software

B) A legitimate software update

C) Malicious software designed to harm or exploit a system

D) A harmless computer program

Answer: - C

8. Which of the following is an example of phishing?

A) Installing antivirus software

B) Sending emails to steal sensitive information

C) Updating your operating system

D) Encrypting files

Answer: - B

9. What is ransomware?

A) Software that boosts computer speed

B) Malware that locks files and demands payment for access

C) An application for secure data transfer

D) A tool for data recovery

Answer: - B

10. How can viruses spread?

A) Through email attachments and infected websites

B) By installing licensed software

C) By using encrypted communication tools

D) Through secure browsing

Answer: - A

11. What is the function of antivirus software?

A) To increase computer processing speed

B) To detect, prevent, and remove malware

C) To create strong passwords

D) To block access to the internet

Answer: - B

12. What is a firewall?

A) A device that stores data

B) A barrier that monitors network traffic for threats

C) A tool for password generation

D) A program for encrypting data

Answer: - B

13. Why is secure browsing important?

A) It improves internet speed

B) It minimizes the risk of online threats like phishing

C) It allows access to all websites

D) It reduces the need for antivirus software

Answer: - B

14. What makes a password strong?

A) Only lowercase letters

B) A combination of uppercase letters, numbers, and symbols

C) The use of common words

D) A password shorter than 6 characters

Answer: - B

15. What is multifactor authentication (MFA)?

A) A method to boost antivirus software

B) A system requiring multiple verification steps for access

C) A tool to recover lost passwords

D) A process for encrypting files

Answer: - B

16. What is ethical hacking?

A) Unauthorized access to networks

B) Testing systems for vulnerabilities to improve security

C) Creating malware for educational purposes

D) Blocking access to websites

Answer: - B

17. What is penetration testing?

A) Testing a system's speed and performance

B) Identifying vulnerabilities in a system

C) Encrypting sensitive data

D) Scanning for viruses

Answer: - B

18. What is the role of ethical hackers?

A) To exploit system vulnerabilities

B) To perform unauthorized network scans

C) To help organizations strengthen their security

D) To distribute malware to test systems

Answer: - C

19. How does ethical hacking differ from malicious hacking?

A) Ethical hacking is unauthorized

B) Ethical hacking improves security, while malicious hacking exploits systems

C) Ethical hacking uses less advanced tools

D) Ethical hacking is only used for testing games

Answer: - B

20. What is the main goal of a security audit?

A) To delete unnecessary files

B) To evaluate and improve a system's security measures

C) To develop new antivirus software

D) To increase system speed

Answer: - B

21. What is programming?

A) Writing instructions for computers to follow

B) Designing hardware components

C) Analyzing large datasets

D) Encrypting sensitive information

Answer: - A

22. What are programs?

A) Physical components of a computer

B) A set of instructions for a computer to execute tasks

C) Antivirus software updates

D) Internet browsing tools

Answer: - B

23. Why do we need programming languages?

A) To encrypt data efficiently

B) To create interactive hardware

C) To communicate instructions to computers

D) To design operating systems

Answer: - C

24. Which of the following best describes programming?

A) Creating art for websites

B) Writing code to instruct computers

C) Designing electronic circuits

D) Debugging hardware components

Answer: - B

25. Which programming language is known for its beginner friendly syntax?

A) Python

B) C++

C) Assembly

D) Java

Answer: - A

26. What is Python commonly used for?

A) Hardware design

B) Web development and data analysis

C) Only game development

D) Writing system firmware

Answer: - B

27. What makes Python beginner friendly?

A) Its complex syntax

B) Its similarity to machine code

C) Its simple and easy to read syntax

D) Its lack of libraries

Answer: - C

Cybersecurity Basics

1. What is the main goal of cybersecurity?

a) Increase internet speed

b) Protect systems and data from attacks

c) Improve computer hardware

d) Create computer games

Answer: - b) Protect systems and data from attacks

2. Which of the following is NOT a key component of cybersecurity?

a) Confidentiality

b) Integrity

c) Speed

d) Availability

Answer: - c) Speed

3. What does a firewall do?

a) Repairs computer hardware

b) Blocks unauthorized access to a network

c) Encrypts data automatically

d) Prevents system updates

Answer: - b) Blocks unauthorized access to a network

4. Why is cybersecurity important for critical infrastructure?

a) To reduce maintenance costs

b) To protect against cyberattacks causing disruptions

c) To improve customer service

d) To increase revenue

Answer: - b) To protect against cyberattacks causing disruptions

5. Which of the following is an example of sensitive information that cybersecurity protects?

a) Birthday parties

b) Banking credentials

c) Public phone directories

d) Weather forecasts

Answer: - b) Banking credentials

2. Common Cybersecurity Threats

6. What is a computer virus?

a) A type of hardware failure

b) A program that selfreplicates and causes harm

c) A security update for software

d) An antivirus application

Answer: - b) A program that self-replicates and causes harm

7. What is the primary purpose of ransomware?

a) To delete all files on a system

b) To encrypt files and demand payment for their release

c) To repair broken system files

d) To protect personal data

Answer: - b) To encrypt files and demand payment for their release

8. Phishing attacks usually involve: -

a) Deleting all user files

b) Sending fake emails to steal sensitive information

c) Blocking system updates

d) Encrypting computer hardware

Answer: - b) Sending fake emails to steal sensitive information

9. Which of the following is NOT malware?

a) Spyware

b) Worm

c) Adware

d) Firewall

Answer: - d) Firewall

10. How can viruses spread to other systems?

a) Through software updates

b) Via infected email attachments

c) Using an antivirus tool

d) Through firewalls

Answer: - b) Via infected email attachments

11. Which of the following is NOT a reason for the importance of cybersecurity?

a) Protecting personal information

b) Preventing financial loss

c) Safeguarding critical infrastructure

d) Reducing software development costs

Answer: - d) Reducing software development costs

12. How does cybersecurity contribute to national security?

a) By reducing the cost of technology

b) By protecting government and military data from cyber threats

c) By increasing internet speed

d) By providing free software updates

Answer: - b) By protecting government and military data from cyber threats

13. What is the consequence of losing trust in online systems due to poor cybersecurity?

a) Increased system efficiency

b) Decrease in customer engagement

c) Reduced software complexity

d) Faster data processing

Answer: - b) Decrease in customer engagement

14. Why is it important to secure medical data?

a) To improve patient recovery time

b) To prevent unauthorized access to sensitive health information

c) To make hospitals more profitable

d) To speed up medical research

Answer: - b) To prevent unauthorized access to sensitive health information

15. What is the role of cybersecurity in business growth?

a) Reducing employee workload

b) Building customer trust through secure systems

c) Increasing the size of the IT department

d) Eliminating the need for software updates

Answer: - b) Building customer trust through secure systems

16. What type of cybersecurity threat can disrupt essential services like water and power?

a) Phishing attacks

b) Attacks on critical infrastructure

c) Adware infections

d) Password theft

Answer: - b) Attacks on critical infrastructure

17. How can cybersecurity prevent identity theft?

a) By encrypting passwords and personal data

b) By increasing software speed

c) By removing all cookies from websites

d) By updating antivirus software weekly

Answer: - a) By encrypting passwords and personal data

18. Which of the following ensures that systems are available to authorized users?

a) Confidentiality

b) Integrity

c) Availability

d) Speed

Answer: - c) Availability

19. Cybersecurity benefits government systems by: -

a) Reducing electricity costs

b) Preventing cyber espionage

c) Offering free cloud storage

d) Automating tax collection

Answer: - b) Preventing cyber espionage

20. Why is cybersecurity critical for online financial transactions?

a) It improves transaction speed

b) It prevents unauthorized access to accounts and payment systems

c) It provides discounts on financial services

d) It removes the need for passwords

Answer: - b) It prevents unauthorized access to accounts and payment systems

21. What is the main goal of phishing attacks?

a) Encrypt data for storage

b) Trick individuals into sharing sensitive information

c) Speed up system performance

d) Remove malware infections

Answer: - b) Trick individuals into sharing sensitive information

22. Which type of malware locks files and demands payment?

a) Worms

b) Spyware

c) Ransomware

d) Adware

Answer: - c) Ransomware

23. Spyware is designed to: -

a) Monitor user activity and steal information

b) Protect sensitive files from hackers

c) Block popup ads

d) Encrypt user data for safety

Answer: - a) Monitor user activity and steal information

24. What differentiates worms from viruses?

a) Worms require user action to spread

b) Worms replicate independently without user action

c) Worms only infect email systems

d) Worms are not considered a threat

Answer: - b) Worms replicate independently without user action

25. Adware often: -

a) Improves system speed

b) Displays unwanted advertisements

c) Deletes files randomly

d) Protects the user from phishing attacks

Answer: - b) Displays unwanted advertisements

26. A Distributed Denial of Service (DDoS) attack aims to: -

a) Steal sensitive information

b) Overwhelm a server to disrupt its services

c) Repair corrupted files

d) Encrypt user data

Answer: - b) Overwhelm a server to disrupt its services

27. Which threat specifically targets users' banking details?

a) Phishing

b) Ransomware

c) Keylogging

d) Spyware

Answer: - c) Keylogging

28. Trojans are disguised as: -

a) Useful programs to deceive users

b) Antivirus software

c) Web browsers

d) Email spam filters

Answer: - a) Useful programs to deceive users

29. What is the primary risk of using public Wi-Fi without protection?

a) Slower internet speeds

b) Increased susceptibility to hacking attacks

c) Excessive battery usage

d) Limited data allowance

Answer: - b) Increased susceptibility to hacking attacks

30. Social engineering attacks rely on: -

a) Exploiting software vulnerabilities

b) Manipulating people to share sensitive information

c) Encrypting system data

d) Increasing malware distribution

Answer: - b) Manipulating people to share sensitive information

Cyber Threats (Continued)

31. What is the purpose of a backdoor in a system?

a) To enhance system performance

b) To allow unauthorized access to the system

c) To encrypt data for security

d) To speed up data transfers

Answer: - b) To allow unauthorized access to the system

32. Zeroday vulnerabilities are: -

a) Issues already patched by software developers

b) Newly discovered vulnerabilities without available fixes

c) Malicious programs installed by users

d) Encrypted data used in ransomware

Answer: - b) Newly discovered vulnerabilities without available fixes

33. Which type of attack captures and analyzes data packets?

a) Phishing

b) Spoofing

c) Man-in-the-middle (MITM) attacks

d) Keylogging

Answer: - c) Man-in-the-middle (MITM) attacks

34. Rootkits are dangerous because they: -

a) Encrypt files to demand ransom

b) Provide attackers with full control of the system

c) Generate random popups

d) Slow down internet speeds

Answer: - b) Provide attackers with full control of the system

35. SQL injection attacks target: -

a) Network firewalls

b) Database vulnerabilities

c) Antivirus programs

d) Operating systems

Answer: - b) Database vulnerabilities

36. Crosssite scripting (XSS) attacks occur when: -

a) Data is encrypted before being stored

b) Malicious scripts are injected into trusted websites

c) Users download unauthorized software

d) Files are corrupted during transfer

Answer: - b) Malicious scripts are injected into trusted websites

37. A botnet is a network of: -

a) Secure devices for data encryption

b) Infected devices controlled by attackers

c) Firewalls that protect systems from attacks

d) Secure servers hosting websites

Answer: - b) Infected devices controlled by attackers

38. What does spyware do?

a) Encrypts files for ransom

b) Steals sensitive information by monitoring user activities

c) Blocks unauthorized emails

d) Repairs damaged files

Answer: - b) Steals sensitive information by monitoring user activities

39. Which attack targets weaknesses in Bluetooth and Wi-Fi connections?

a) SQL injection

b) Network spoofing

c) Bluejacking

d) Packet sniffing

Answer: - c) Bluejacking

40. What is the primary risk of phishing emails?

a) Slow computer performance

b) Unauthorized access to sensitive data

c) Overuse of system memory

d) Loss of internet connection

Answer: - b) Unauthorized access to sensitive data

41. What is the role of antivirus software?

a) To delete unwanted files

b) To detect, prevent, and remove malware

c) To improve internet speed

d) To block advertisements

Answer: - b) To detect, prevent, and remove malware

42. How does a firewall enhance security?

a) By improving system performance

b) By monitoring and blocking unauthorized traffic

c) By encrypting user files

d) By providing free updates to software

Answer: - b) By monitoring and blocking unauthorized traffic

43. A secure website can be identified by: -

a) The presence of "http" in the URL

b) A padlock icon and "https" in the URL

c) A warning message before loading

d) A faster loading time

Answer: - b) A padlock icon and "https" in the URL

44. What does multifactor authentication (MFA) require?

a) Only a strong password

b) Multiple levels of user identification

c) A firewall and antivirus software

d) Biometric verification only

Answer: - b) Multiple levels of user identification

45. Regular software updates are essential because they: -

a) Improve system aesthetics

b) Fix known vulnerabilities and enhance security

c) Remove unused applications

d) Increase computer speed permanently

Answer: - b) Fix known vulnerabilities and enhance security

46. Which of the following helps prevent phishing attacks?

a) Opening all attachments in emails

b) Verifying email sources before clicking links

c) Using unsecured websites

d) Avoiding antivirus software

Answer: - b) Verifying email sources before clicking links

47. Why is it important to use strong, unique passwords?

a) To reduce system memory usage

b) To make it difficult for attackers to guess or crack them

c) To prevent software updates

d) To speed up login processes

Answer: - b) To make it difficult for attackers to guess or crack them

48. Encrypted communication prevents: -

a) Data transfer between devices

b) Unauthorized access to data during transmission

c) Secure connections over private networks

d) Software installation errors

Answer: - b) Unauthorized access to data during transmission

49. A Virtual Private Network (VPN) is used to: -

a) Block all malware

b) Create a secure, encrypted connection over the internet

c) Prevent spam emails

d) Increase internet speed

Answer: - b) Create a secure, encrypted connection over the internet

50. Why is it necessary to backup data regularly?

a) To improve system performance

b) To ensure data recovery in case of loss or attack

c) To reduce the need for software updates

d) To save storage space

Answer: - b) To ensure data recovery in case of loss or attack

51. Which of the following is an example of biometric authentication?

a) Password entry

b) Fingerprint scanning

c) CAPTCHA verification

d) Security questions

Answer: - b) Fingerprint scanning

52. Twofactor authentication (2FA) typically combines: -

a) A password and a personal identification number (PIN)

b) Something you know (password) and something you have (security token)

c) Biometrics and CAPTCHA verification

d) Firewall and antivirus software

Answer: - b) Something you know (password) and something you have (security token)

53. How can you avoid ransomware attacks?

a) Avoid opening unsolicited email attachments

b) Use unsecured networks

c) Disable antivirus software

d) Share passwords freely

Answer: - a) Avoid opening unsolicited email attachments

54. Software patches are: -

a) Temporary fixes for system crashes

b) Updates to fix vulnerabilities and improve software functionality

c) Backup tools for data recovery

d) Firewalls for network security

Answer: - b) Updates to fix vulnerabilities and improve software functionality

55. Why should public WiFi be used cautiously?

a) It is always slow and unreliable

b) It can expose data to potential attackers due to lack of encryption

c) It blocks secure websites

d) It disables antivirus programs

Answer: - b) It can expose data to potential attackers due to lack of encryption

56. What is the role of a spam filter in email security?

a) To enhance email loading speeds

b) To detect and block potentially harmful or unwanted emails

c) To encrypt all outgoing emails

d) To organize emails into folders

Answer: - b) To detect and block potentially harmful or unwanted emails

57. Which tool can protect your network from unauthorized access?

a) Firewall

b) VPN

c) Data backup

d) Encryption software

Answer: - a) Firewall

58. Browser extensions can enhance security by: -

a) Automatically downloading files

b) Blocking popups and trackers

c) Disabling secure websites

d) Increasing browsing speed

Answer: - b) Blocking popups and trackers

59. What is phishing simulation training?

a) Software that blocks phishing emails

b) Training employees to recognize and avoid phishing attempts

c) Testing new phishing attack methods

d) Creating phishing emails to share internally

Answer: - b) Training employees to recognize and avoid phishing attempts

60. A key feature of secure cloud storage services is: -

a) Unlimited storage space

b) Regular encryption of stored data

c) Higher download speeds

d) Automatic installation of applications

Answer: - b) Regular encryption of stored data

61. Using outdated software increases the risk of: -

a) Faster processing speeds

b) Compatibility issues and cyber vulnerabilities

c) Enhanced graphics performance

d) Improved data encryption

Answer: - b) Compatibility issues and cyber vulnerabilities

62. Data loss prevention (DLP) tools are used to: -

a) Recover deleted files

b) Prevent sensitive information from being shared outside an organization

c) Speed up system performance

d) Analyze network traffic

Answer: - b) Prevent sensitive information from being shared outside an organization

63. What is an intrusion detection system (IDS)?

a) Software that monitors and detects unauthorized access to networks

b) Hardware to boost system performance

c) Antivirus that removes malware

d) A tool for encrypting sensitive data

Answer: - a) Software that monitors and detects unauthorized access to networks

64. Password managers help by: -

a) Generating and storing strong, unique passwords

b) Speeding up login processes

c) Preventing system crashes

d) Sharing passwords across multiple users

Answer: - a) Generating and storing strong, unique passwords

65. What is the benefit of using a private DNS server?

a) Faster website loading times

b) Enhanced privacy and reduced tracking by ISPs

c) Automatic firewall configuration

d) Increased file download speeds

Answer: - b) Enhanced privacy and reduced tracking by ISPs

66. What does "sandboxing" mean in cybersecurity?

a) Running unknown programs in a controlled environment to observe their behavior

b) Encrypting all user data for secure storage

c) Blocking access to unverified websites

d) Partitioning hard drives for better organization

Answer: - a) Running unknown programs in a controlled environment to observe their behavior

67. How does updating firmware help with security?

a) Increases device speed

b) Fixes bugs and vulnerabilities in hardware devices

c) Removes unnecessary applications

d) Simplifies system settings

Answer: - b) Fixes bugs and vulnerabilities in hardware devices

68. What is the role of an encryption algorithm?

a) To speed up system processes

b) To protect data by converting it into unreadable formats

c) To enhance user interfaces

d) To detect malware on a system

Answer: - b) To protect data by converting it into unreadable formats

69. Which security measure can prevent brute force attacks?

a) Limiting login attempts

b) Using outdated software

c) Allowing multiple password retries

d) Disabling firewalls

Answer: - a) Limiting login attempts

70. Physical security measures for cybersecurity include: -

a) Installing antivirus software

b) Using strong passwords

c) Restricting access to hardware and server rooms

d) Encrypting network traffic

Answer: - c) Restricting access to hardware and server rooms

71. What is ethical hacking?

a) Unauthorized access to systems for personal gain

b) Authorized testing of systems for vulnerabilities

c) Disabling firewalls to access sensitive data

d) Developing new viruses for research

Answer: - b) Authorized testing of systems for vulnerabilities

72. Ethical hackers are also known as: -

a) Greyhat hackers

b) Blackhat hackers

c) Whitehat hackers

d) Script kiddies

Answer: - c) Whitehat hackers

73. The primary purpose of penetration testing is to: -

a) Steal sensitive information

b) Fix system performance issues

c) Identify and fix security vulnerabilities

d) Improve network speed

Answer: - c) Identify and fix security vulnerabilities

Ethical Hacking (Continued)

74. Which organization is most likely to hire an ethical hacker?

a) A criminal group

b) A government agency or corporation

c) A private individual

d) A social media influencer

Answer: - b) A government agency or corporation

75. What does a vulnerability assessment involve?

a) Writing malicious code

b) Identifying and ranking potential system weaknesses

c) Testing system performance

d) Disabling antivirus software

Answer: - b) Identifying and ranking potential system weaknesses

76. What is the key difference between blackhat and whitehat hackers?

a) Blackhat hackers work legally, while whitehat hackers do not

b) Blackhat hackers exploit vulnerabilities, while whitehat hackers fix them

c) Blackhat hackers only target companies, while whitehat hackers target individuals

d) Blackhat hackers use older tools compared to whitehat hackers

Answer: - b) Blackhat hackers exploit vulnerabilities, while whitehat hackers fix them

77. What is the first step in ethical hacking?

a) Exploiting vulnerabilities

b) Scanning the target system

c) Reconnaissance or gathering information

d) Reporting to law enforcement

Answer: - c) Reconnaissance or gathering information

78. During penetration testing, what is privilege escalation?

a) Moving from a lower to a higher level of access within a system

b) Granting other users unauthorized access

c) Removing admin rights from authorized users

d) Blocking unauthorized access attempts

Answer: - a) Moving from a lower to a higher level of access within a system

79. Which tool is commonly used in ethical hacking?

a) Metasploit

b) Microsoft Excel

c) Adobe Photoshop

d) Zoom

Answer: - a) Metasploit

80. Ethical hackers must adhere to: -

a) Their personal goals

b) Industry and organizational ethical guidelines

c) Blackhat hacking principles

d) Government hacking laws only

Answer: - b) Industry and organizational ethical guidelines

81. Which of the following describes penetration testing?

a) Creating a firewall for a network

b) Testing a system to find security vulnerabilities

c) Writing malicious software

d) Hacking into random systems

Answer: - b) Testing a system to find security vulnerabilities

82. Social engineering attacks can be tested by ethical hackers to: -

a) Manipulate employees to reveal sensitive information

b) Create fake websites for phishing purposes

c) Evaluate an organization's human security weaknesses

d) Disrupt online services

Answer: - c) Evaluate an organization's human security weaknesses

83. What is a black box penetration test?

a) Testing with full knowledge of the system

b) Testing with no prior knowledge of the system

c) Testing with a team of external hackers

d) Testing using only network-based tools

Answer: - b) Testing with no prior knowledge of the system

84. Which document authorizes ethical hackers to perform tests?

a) Enduser agreement

b) Nondisclosure agreement

c) Penetration testing contract or "Rules of Engagement"

d) Confidentiality waiver

Answer: - c) Penetration testing contract or "Rules of Engagement"

85. Ethical hacking tools must be used: -

a) Only for authorized purposes

b) For testing without permission

c) To bypass firewalls

d) To attack competing organizations

Answer: - a) Only for authorized purposes

86. A red team in ethical hacking is responsible for: -

a) Monitoring and responding to hacking attempts

b) Actively simulating attacks on systems

c) Training employees in cybersecurity

d) Designing firewalls

Answer: - b) Actively simulating attacks on systems

87. Which type of ethical hacking focuses on testing network vulnerabilities?

a) Web application hacking

b) Network penetration testing

c) Wireless security testing

d) Social engineering

Answer: - b) Network penetration testing

88. Reconnaissance during ethical hacking involves: -

a) Launching malware

b) Gathering information about the target system

c) Deleting sensitive data

d) Breaking into the system

Answer: - b) Gathering information about the target system

89. What is a common legal concern with ethical hacking?

a) Breaching systems without explicit permission

b) Using outdated hacking tools

c) Failing to identify all vulnerabilities

d) Overreporting security weaknesses

Answer: - a) Breaching systems without explicit permission

90. A white box penetration test means: -

a) Testing with limited access to system details

b) Testing with full access and knowledge of the system

c) Using only automated tools

d) Only testing external networks

Answer: - b) Testing with full access and knowledge of the system

91. What is the primary purpose of a bug bounty program?

a) To reward ethical hackers for identifying security vulnerabilities

b) To encourage hacking for personal gain

c) To reduce the cost of software development

d) To eliminate the need for antivirus software

Answer: - a) To reward ethical hackers for identifying security vulnerabilities

92. Wireless penetration testing focuses on: -

a) Testing the strength of wired networks

b) Evaluating vulnerabilities in Wi-Fi networks

c) Scanning physical devices for malware

d) Tracking unauthorized devices

Answer: - b) Evaluating vulnerabilities in Wi-Fi networks

93. The term "zero-day vulnerability" refers to: -

a) A bug that has been patched

b) A vulnerability that is unknown to the software developer

c) A virus affecting only outdated systems

d) A threat that only impacts mobile devices

Answer: - b) A vulnerability that is unknown to the software developer

94. Ethical hackers need to have strong knowledge of: -

a) Cybersecurity laws, coding, and system architecture

b) Web design and user interfaces

c) Only data entry processes

d) Mobile application trends

Answer: - a) Cybersecurity laws, coding, and system architecture

95. Greyhat hackers: -

a) Always act with malicious intent

b) May hack systems without permission but do not exploit vulnerabilities

c) Are only interested in financial gains

d) Work solely for governments

Answer: - b) May hack systems without permission but do not exploit vulnerabilities

96. Ethical hacking certifications, such as CEH, are important because: -

a) They guarantee financial rewards

b) They provide credibility and recognized skills in cybersecurity

c) They eliminate the need for practical experience

d) They are mandatory for all software developers

Answer: - b) They provide credibility and recognized skills in cybersecurity

97. A backdoor in cybersecurity refers to: -

a) A physical entry point to a server room

b) A hidden method for bypassing security measures

c) A legitimate method for granting user permissions

d) A secondary network interface

Answer: - b) A hidden method for bypassing security measures

98. What is the final step in ethical hacking?

a) Exploiting vulnerabilities

b) Writing a detailed report of findings and recommendations

c) Breaking into additional systems

d) Deleting evidence of testing

Answer: - b) Writing a detailed report of findings and recommendations

99. What is the role of blue teams in ethical hacking?

a) Simulating cyberattacks on systems

b) Defending systems against real or simulated attacks

c) Designing malware for testing

d) Testing physical security measures

Answer: - b) Defending systems against real or simulated attacks

100. Ethical hacking benefits organizations by: -

a) Reducing their overall IT budget

b) Proactively identifying and fixing vulnerabilities before cybercriminals exploit them

c) Allowing employees to bypass security protocols

d) Sharing sensitive data with ethical hackers

Answer: - b) Proactively identifying and fixing vulnerabilities before cybercriminals exploit them

101. Which of the following is a basic concept in programming?

a) Memory management

b) Cloud computing

c) Multithreading

d) Recursion

Answer: - d) Recursion

102. What is the purpose of a variable in programming?

a) To store data temporarily

b) To perform mathematical operations

c) To create loops

d) To print output

Answer: - a) To store data temporarily

103. Which of these is an example of a high-level programming language?

a) Assembly

b) C

c) Python

d) Machine code

Answer: - c) Python

104. In object-oriented programming, what does the term "inheritance" refer to?

a) Reusing existing code to create new classes

b) Storing data in a database

c) Running multiple threads simultaneously

d) Encrypting sensitive information

Answer: - a) Reusing existing code to create new classes

105. What is an algorithm in programming?

a) A set of instructions to solve a problem

b) A type of programming language

c) A software library for managing memory

d) A command to execute a program

Answer: - a) A set of instructions to solve a problem

106. What does the term "debugging" mean in programming?

a) Writing new code

b) Finding and fixing errors in the code

c) Compiling the code

d) Designing the user interface

Answer: - b) Finding and fixing errors in the code

107. What is the purpose of a loop in programming?

a) To store data

b) To repeat a block of code multiple times

c) To handle errors

d) To create user interfaces

Answer: - b) To repeat a block of code multiple times

108. What does the "if" statement do in a program?

a) Creates a loop

b) Checks a condition and executes code based on the result

c) Stores a value

d) Defines a function

Answer: - b) Checks a condition and executes code based on the result

109. Which data structure is typically used to store keyvalue pairs?

a) Array

b) Stack

c) Queue

d) Dictionary

Answer: - d) Dictionary

110. What is the purpose of a function in programming?

a) To store values

b) To break the program into smaller, reusable blocks of code

c) To design the layout of a program

d) To execute the program

Answer: - b) To break the program into smaller, reusable blocks of code

111. Which of the following is not an interpreted programming language?

a) Python

b) JavaScript

c) C++

d) Ruby

Answer: - c) C++

112. Which programming language is primarily used for developing Android applications?

a) Swift

b) Java

c) Kotlin

d) C

Answer: - b) Java

113. Which programming language is known for its use in web development on the client side?

a) Python

b) JavaScript

c) C

d) Ruby

Answer: - b) JavaScript

114. What is the main purpose of the C programming language?

a) Web development

b) System programming and hardware access

c) Artificial intelligence

d) Mobile application development

Answer: - b) System programming and hardware access

115. Which language is primarily used for machine learning and data science applications?

a) C++

b) Python

c) JavaScript

d) HTML

Answer: - b) Python

116. What type of language is Swift?

a) Procedural programming language

b) Objectoriented programming language

c) Scripting language

d) Assembly language

Answer: - b) Objectoriented programming language

117. What language is commonly used for web development on the server side?

a) Ruby

b) C

c) PHP

d) JavaScript

Answer: - c) PHP

118. Which of the following languages is used for iOS app development?

a) Kotlin

b) Swift

c) Java

d) C

Answer: - b) Swift

119. Ruby is most commonly associated with which web development framework?

a) Laravel

b) Angular

c) Ruby on Rails

d) Django

Answer: - c) Ruby on Rails

120. Which language is known for its use in data manipulation and statistical analysis?

a) Java

b) R

c) Go

d) C++

Answer: - b) R

121. Which programming language is primarily used for developing cross-platform mobile applications?

a) Java

b) Kotlin

c) React Native

d) ObjectiveC

Answer: - c) React Native

122. The programming language Java was designed for: -

a) Web development only

b) Cross-platform compatibility

c) Hardware Programming

d) Mobile applications

Answer: - b) Cross-platform compatibility

123. Which of these languages is considered a low-level programming language?

a) Python

b) JavaScript

c) C

d) Assembly

Answer: - d) Assembly

124. Which language is most often used for developing high-performance applications and games?

a) JavaScript

b) C

c) C++

d) Python

Answer: - c) C++

125. What programming language is the core language for Android app development?

a) Kotlin

b) Swift

c) Ruby

d) Java

Answer: - a) Kotlin

126. The Java programming language follows which programming paradigm?

a) Functional programming

b) Object-oriented programming

c) Procedural programming

d) Logic programming

Answer: - b) Object-oriented programming

127. Which programming language is commonly used for web development with Django framework?

a) Python

b) PHP

c) Ruby

d) Java

Answer: - a) Python

128. Which of the following is a feature of C++ over C?

a) Object-oriented programming features

b) Faster execution speed

c) Simpler syntax

d) Simpler memory management

Answer: - a) Object-oriented programming features

129. What is the main characteristic of scripting languages like JavaScript and Python?

a) They require compiling before execution

b) They are executed directly from the source code

c) They can only run in specific environments

d) They are designed for low-level programming

Answer: - b) They are executed directly from the source code

130. What is the primary purpose of the Go programming language (Golang)?

a) Web development

b) System level programming

c) Scientific computing

d) Cloud computing and microservices

Answer: - d) Cloud computing and microservices

131. What is the first step in debugging a program?

a) Fixing the errors

b) Identifying where the issue occurs

c) Writing new test cases

d) Rewriting the entire code

Answer: - b) Identifying where the issue occurs

132. What does a "syntax error" mean in programming?

a) A logical mistake in the code

b) The program doesn't compile due to incorrect code structure

c) The code runs but produces incorrect output

d) The program encounters an exception during execution

Answer: - b) The program doesn't compile due to incorrect code structure

133. What is the purpose of a debugger in programming?

a) To run the program automatically

b) To test code execution at runtime

c) To identify and fix syntax errors

d) To generate reports for endusers

Answer: - b) To test code execution at runtime

134. What is the significance of breakpoints in debugging?

a) They stop the program from running

b) They pause the program at specific points to examine variables and flow

c) They remove errors automatically

d) They skip over sections of the code

Answer: - b) They pause the program at specific points to examine variables and flow

135. What is the purpose of "logging" in debugging?

a) To print the final result

b) To display information about the program's execution for troubleshooting

c) To execute the code

d) To create backups of the program

Answer: - b) To display information about the program's execution for troubleshooting

136. What does the term "unit testing" refer to in programming?

a) Testing an entire system

b) Testing small, individual units or components of the program

c) Testing user interface components

d) Testing network security

Answer: - b) Testing small, individual units or components of the program

137. In what scenario would you use the "step over" function in debugging?

a) To skip over a function call and move to the next line of code

b) To skip over lines of code that are unnecessary

c) To pause the program and inspect the memory

d) To execute a specific part of the code multiple times

Answer: - a) To skip over a function call and move to the next line of code

138. What is an "exception" in programming?

a) A function that handles errors

b) A special kind of error that occurs during program execution

c) A method that outputs results

d) A feature that prevents bugs from happening

Answer: - b) A special kind of error that occurs during program execution

139. What is "refactoring" in the context of programming?

a) Changing the design of the user interface

b) Altering the code to improve readability or performance without changing its behavior

c) Fixing syntax errors

d) Writing new test cases for a function

Answer: - b) Altering the code to improve readability or performance without changing its behavior

140. In debugging, what does "step into" do?

a) It skips over a function call

b) It lets the program run to the next breakpoint

c) It enters the function being called and lets you debug it line by line

d) It compiles the entire code

Answer: - c) It enters the function being called and lets you debug it line by line

141. What is the purpose of using a "watch" in debugging?

a) To monitor changes in the program's execution time

b) To track the value of specific variables during execution

c) To run the program on multiple devices

d) To measure the memory usage of the program

Answer: - b) To track the value of specific variables during execution

142. What does "stack trace" refer to in programming?

a) The sequence of function calls that lead to an error or exception

b) The memory allocation of the program

c) The list of all variables used in the program

d) A list of all the program's input and output data

Answer: - a) The sequence of function calls that lead to an error or exception

143. When is "code profiling" most commonly used?

a) To ensure that the code is syntactically correct

b) To find performance bottlenecks in the program

c) To write documentation for the code

d) To test user input for errors

Answer: - b) To find performance bottlenecks in the program

144. Which of the following is a common technique for detecting memory leaks?

a) Code profiling

b) Memory allocation

c) Stack overflow

d) Heap analysis

Answer: - a) Code profiling

145. What is the purpose of "code coverage" in testing?

a) To ensure the program is free from bugs

b) To measure how much of the code is tested during unit testing

c) To optimize the code for performance

d) To check the user interface for errors

Answer: - b) To measure how much of the code is tested during unit testing

146. Which of these is the primary goal of "exception handling" in programming?

a) To automatically fix errors in the code

b) To gracefully handle runtime errors and ensure the program doesn’t crash

c) To optimize memory usage

d) To generate user documentation

Answer: - b) To gracefully handle runtime errors and ensure the program doesn’t crash

147. What is a "segmentation fault"?

a) An error caused by incorrect memory access

b) A logical error in the code

c) A syntax error in the program

d) A user input error

Answer: - a) An error caused by incorrect memory access

148. What is the advantage of using "unit tests" for debugging?

a) They help find bugs in specific functions or units of the program

b) They speed up the development process

c) They fix memory leaks automatically

d) They run the entire system to test for errors

Answer: - a) They help find bugs in specific functions or units of the program

149. What does "assertion" in programming typically check for?

a) Syntax errors in the program

b) Logic errors in the program

c) Conditions that should always be true during execution

d) Memory usage of the program

Answer: - c) Conditions that should always be true during execution

150. What is a "deadlock" in multithreading?

a) A situation where two or more threads are waiting for each other to release resources, causing a program to stop

b) An error in the memory allocation process

c) A bug caused by improper exception handling

d) A failure in the network communication between threads

Answer: - a) A situation where two or more threads are waiting for each other to release resources, causing a program to stop

151. Which of the following is the best strategy for debugging large programs?

a) Use only print statements for debugging

b) Implement a step-by-step approach with breakpoints and logging

c) Run the entire program multiple times without making changes

d) Rebuild the program from scratch

Answer: - b) Implement a step-by-step approach with breakpoints and logging

152. How do "try catch" blocks help in exception handling?

a) By allowing the program to ignore errors and continue

b) By preventing errors from occurring

c) By providing a way to catch and handle exceptions when they occur

d) By automatically fixing the error

Answer: - c) By providing a way to catch and handle exceptions when they occur

153. What is the main difference between a "runtime error" and a "compile time error"?

a) Runtime errors occur during program execution, while compile time errors occur when the program is being compiled

b) Runtime errors can't be fixed, while compile time errors can be fixed easily

c) Runtime errors happen only in interpreted languages, while compile time errors happen in compiled languages

d) Runtime errors are caused by incorrect logic, while compile time errors are caused by incorrect syntax

Answer: - a) Runtime errors occur during program execution, while compile time errors occur when the program is being compiled

154. What is the purpose of using "assert" in debugging?

a) To print variables to the console

b) To force the program to exit when an error is detected

c) To check for specific conditions in the code and raise an exception if the condition is false

d) To optimize code execution

Answer: - c) To check for specific conditions in the code and raise an exception if the condition is false

155. What is the purpose of a "memory dump" during debugging?

a) To show the program's variables and their values at a specific point in time

b) To free up memory resources

c) To check for memory leaks

d) To restart the program

Answer: - a) To show the program's variables and their values at a specific point in time

156. What does "stack overflow" refer to in programming?

a) A buffer overflow error

b) An error caused by using too much memory on the stack

c) An exception caused by incorrect data types

d) A failure in the program's flow control

Answer: - b) An error caused by using too much memory on the stack

157. What tool is commonly used to measure code performance?

a) Compiler

b) Profiler

c) Debugger

d) Editor

Answer: - b) Profiler

158. What does "integration testing" refer to?

a) Testing individual functions in isolation

b) Testing the interaction between different modules or components of a system

c) Testing user interfaces

d) Testing memory usage

Answer: - b) Testing the interaction between different modules or components of a system

159. What is the primary goal of "static code analysis"?

a) To check for runtime errors

b) To evaluate code performance

c) To identify potential bugs and vulnerabilities without executing the program

d) To compile the code

Answer: - c) To identify potential bugs and vulnerabilities without executing the program

160. What is a common cause of "infinite loops" in programming?

a) Incorrect variable initialization

b) The loop condition never becoming false

c) Missing parentheses in the code

d) Incorrect function parameters

Answer: - b) The loop condition never becoming false

161. What is an example of "real-time processing" in programming?

a) Sorting a large dataset for analysis

b) Playing an online game with multiple players in real time

c) Compiling a program

d) Generating reports from a database

Answer: - b) Playing an online game with multiple players in real time

162. What is the main purpose of "database indexing"?

a) To store user data

b) To optimize query performance by reducing the amount of data to scan

c) To increase the data redundancy in the database

d) To create backup copies of the database

Answer: - b) To optimize query performance by reducing the amount of data to scan

163. How does "cloud computing" benefit programming applications?

a) By storing all code locally for faster execution

b) By providing scalable infrastructure and services without requiring on-premise hardware

c) By automatically fixing bugs in the code

d) By allowing developers to write code offline

Answer: - b) By providing scalable infrastructure and services without requiring on-premise hardware

164. What is the purpose of "data encryption" in practical applications?

a) To speed up program execution

b) To ensure that sensitive data is protected and secure during transmission

c) To reduce the size of data files

d) To improve data query performance

Answer: - b) To ensure that sensitive data is protected and secure during transmission

165. What type of application would most benefit from "asynchronous programming"?

a) A simple calculator application

b) A web server handling multiple requests at the same time

c) A video editor that processes video clips

d) A command-line script that runs one task at a time

Answer: - b) A web server handling multiple requests at the same time

166. Which of these programming paradigms is commonly used for creating user interfaces?

a) Functional programming

b) Object-oriented programming

c) Procedural programming

d) Logic programming

Answer: - b) Object-oriented programming

167. What is the advantage of "containerization" in software deployment?

a) It ensures faster code execution

b) It simplifies the creation of virtual machines

c) It allows applications to run consistently across different computing environments

d) It automates bug fixing

Answer: - c) It allows applications to run consistently across different computing environments

168. How does "DevOps" benefit the software development process?

a) By separating the development and operations teams

b) By automating the process of building, testing, and deploying code

c) By focusing on only manual testing

d) By removing the need for version control

Answer: - b) By automating the process of building, testing, and deploying code

169. What is a typical use case for "blockchain technology" in practical applications?

a) Data encryption

b) Secure and decentralized transaction processing

c) Data analysis

d) Realtime video streaming

Answer: - b) Secure and decentralized transaction processing

170. What does "load balancing" refer to in the context of web applications?

a) Splitting the database into multiple partitions

b) Distributing incoming traffic across multiple servers to ensure no single server is overwhelmed

c) Automatically adjusting server configurations for better performance

d) Encrypting data between servers

Answer: - b) Distributing incoming traffic across multiple servers to ensure no single server is overwhelmed

171. How does "machine learning" apply to practical applications?

a) By automating the testing of programs

b) By allowing computers to learn from data and make decisions without explicit programming

c) By reducing the amount of code needed to create a program

d) By optimizing hardware performance

Answer: - b) By allowing computers to learn from data and make decisions without explicit programming

172. What is "continuous integration" in software development?

a) A method of integrating code into the main branch after each change is made

b) A process where code is tested manually before integration

c) A practice of integrating new features only at the end of the project

d) A way to integrate multiple programming languages into one codebase

Answer: - a) A method of integrating code into the main branch after each change is made

173. What is an example of a "real-time database"?

a) A database storing historical financial data

b) A database used for storing static files like images

c) A database that updates instantly with changes in real-world events, such as stock market prices

d) A database used for data analytics

Answer: - c) A database that updates instantly with changes in realworld events, such as stock market prices

174. What is the purpose of "API (Application Programming Interface)" in modern software applications?

a) To provide a user interface for interaction

b) To enable different software applications to communicate with each other

c) To store user data

d) To handle memory management

Answer: - b) To enable different software applications to communicate with each other

175. In the context of practical programming applications, what is a "microservice"?

a) A small library used for testing

b) A large, monolithic application

c) A small, independent service that handles a specific task in a larger system

d) A protocol used for data transfer

Answer: - c) A small, independent service that handles a specific task in a larger system

Microsoft Office: -

1. What is the purpose of using templates in MS Office?

a) To delete files

b) To quickly create professional looking documents

c) To run antivirus scans

d) To close the application

Answer: - b) To quickly create professional looking documents

2. Which feature allows multiple users to edit the same document in real time in MS Office?

a) Track Changes

b) Cloud Computing

c) Collaborative Features

d) Print Preview

Answer: - c) Collaborative Features

3. What is the purpose of macros in MS Office?

a) To speed up computer performance

b) To automate repetitive tasks

c) To enhance visual appeal

d) To enable antivirus scans

Answer: - b) To automate repetitive tasks

4. Which MS Office tool is best for creating a business presentation?

a) MS Word

b) MS Excel

c) MS PowerPoint

d) MS Access

Answer: - c) MS PowerPoint

5. Which shortcut is used to undo the last action in MS Office?

a) Ctrl + S

b) Ctrl + Y

c) Ctrl + Z

d) Ctrl + P

Answer: - c) Ctrl + Z

Flowcharts and ProblemSolving

6. Which symbol is used to represent a decision in a flowchart?

a) Oval

b) Rectangle

c) Diamond

d) Parallelogram

Answer: - c) Diamond

7. What is the primary purpose of a flowchart?

a) To create presentations

b) To visually represent a process

c) To write code

d) To store data

Answer: - b) To visually represent a process

8. What step comes after identifying a problem when creating a flowchart?

a) Testing the solution

b) Reviewing the process

c) Defining the steps

d) Using appropriate symbols

Answer: - c) Defining the steps

9. Which symbol in a flowchart is used for input/output operations?

a) Oval

b) Parallelogram

c) Rectangle

d) Diamond

Answer: - b) Parallelogram

10. What is the key advantage of using flowcharts in problem-solving?

a) Saves storage space

b) Eliminates programming

c) Simplifies complex tasks into manageable parts

d) Speeds up hardware operations

Answer: - c) Simplifies complex tasks into manageable parts

Computer Shortcut Keys

11. What does Ctrl + F do in most applications?

a) Opens the Find function

b) Saves the document

c) Copies selected text

d) Closes the application

Answer: - a) Opens the Find function

12. Which shortcut allows you to switch between open applications?

a) Alt + Tab

b) Ctrl + A

c) Ctrl + Z

d) Alt + F4

Answer: - a) Alt + Tab

13. What is the function of Ctrl + P?

a) Paste the copied item

b) Print the current document

c) Save the file

d) Open the Find dialog box

Answer: - b) Print the current document

14. Which shortcut key is used to select all items on the screen?

a) Ctrl + V

b) Ctrl + A

c) Ctrl + Z

d) Ctrl + X

Answer: - b) Ctrl + A

15. What does Alt + F4 do?

a) Opens a new tab

b) Saves the document

c) Closes the current application

d) Cuts the selected text

Answer: - c) Closes the current application

Viruses and Cyber Threats

16. Which of the following is NOT a type of malware?

a) Virus

b) Worm

c) Trojan

d) Firewall

Answer: - d) Firewall

17. What type of malware locks files and demands payment to unlock them?

a) Virus

b) Ransomware

c) Trojan

d) Worm

Answer: - b) Ransomware

18. What is the primary function of antivirus software?

a) To edit documents

b) To protect systems from malware

c) To increase internet speed

d) To backup files

Answer: - b) To protect systems from malware

19. Which of the following is a common way viruses spread?

a) Clicking on suspicious email links

b) Installing operating system updates

c) Using official antivirus software

d) Accessing secure websites

Answer: - a) Clicking on suspicious email links

20. What should you regularly do to protect important files from ransomware?

a) Use a weak password

b) Share files online

c) Backup your files

d) Ignore software updates

Answer: - c) Backup your files

Computer Networking Basics

21. What does IP stand for in networking?

a) Internet Protocol

b) Internal Processing

c) Interconnected Path

d) Input Program

Answer: - a) Internet Protocol

22. Which device is used to connect multiple computers in a network?

a) Printer

b) Switch

c) Monitor

d) Scanner

Answer: - b) Switch

23. What is the full form of LAN?

a) Local Area Network

b) Large Access Node

c) Linked Access Network

d) Logical Application Network

Answer: - a) Local Area Network

24. Which of the following is an example of a wireless network?

a) Ethernet

b) Wi-Fi

c) Optical fiber

d) DSL

Answer: - b) Wi-Fi

25. What is the purpose of a firewall in networking?

a) To enhance internet speed

b) To prevent unauthorized access

c) To store data

d) To control server settings

Answer: - b) To prevent unauthorized access

Operating Systems

26. What is the primary role of an operating system?

a) Manage hardware and software resources

b) Design web pages

c) Edit photos

d) Increase computer speed

Answer: - a) Manage hardware and software resources

27. Which of the following is NOT an operating system?

a) Linux

b) macOS

c) MS Excel

d) Windows

Answer: - c) MS Excel

28. What does GUI stand for in operating systems?

a) Graphical User Interaction

b) General User Interface

c) Graphical User Interface

d) General Usage Integration

Answer: - c) Graphical User Interface

29. Which of the following is an open-source operating system?

a) Windows

b) macOS

c) Linux

d) Android

Answer: - c) Linux

30. What is the function of the Task Manager in Windows?

a) Design databases

b) Track running processes and system performance

c) Provide antivirus protection

d) Schedule meetings

Answer: - b) Track running processes and system performance

31. What is the term for a mistake in a program?

a) Bug

b) Patch

c) Module

d) Syntax

Answer: - a) Bug

32. Which programming language is primarily used for web development?

a) Python

b) JavaScript

c) C++

d) Assembly Language

Answer: - b) JavaScript

33. What is the output of 2 + 2 *3 in most programming languages?

a) 12

b) 8

c) 10

d) 6

Answer: - b) 8

34. What does "loop" mean in programming?

a) An error in the program

b) A repeated sequence of instructions

c) A function call

d) A method of debugging

Answer: - b) A repeated sequence of instructions

35. What does the term "variable" mean in programming?

a) A fixed value in the code

b) A name that stores data

c) A type of error

d) A loop structure

Answer: - b) A name that stores data

36. What is a database?

a) A system to store and manage data

b) A type of software for editing photos

c) A collection of unrelated files

d) A system to browse the internet

Answer: - a) A system to store and manage data

37. Which of the following is an example of a relational database management system (RDBMS)?

a) MS Word

b) MySQL

c) Photoshop

d) Notepad

Answer: - b) MySQL

38. What does SQL stand for?

a) Simple Query Language

b) Structured Query Language

c) Standard Query Link

d) Sequential Query Language

Answer: - b) Structured Query Language

39. What is a table in a database?

a) A chart used for analysis

b) A collection of rows and columns to store data

c) A list of commands

d) A design for web pages

Answer: - b) A collection of rows and columns to store data

40. Which of the following is a unique identifier for a record in a database table?

a) Primary Key

b) Foreign Key

c) Column Key

d) Secondary Key

Answer: - a) Primary Key

Digital Communication

41. What does the term "CC" stand for in emails?

a) Carbon Copy

b) Content Check

c) Creative Content

d) Communication Channel

Answer: - a) Carbon Copy

42. What is phishing?

a) A technique for enhancing internet speed

b) A method of stealing sensitive information via fake websites or emails

c) A type of programming loop

d) A method of compressing data

Answer: - b) A method of stealing sensitive information via fake websites or emails

43. Which protocol is commonly used for sending emails?

a) FTP

b) SMTP

c) HTTP

d) DNS

Answer: - b) SMTP

44. What does the term "attachment" refer to in an email?

a) A text format

b) A file sent along with the email

c) A shortcut key

d) An email subject line

Answer: - b) A file sent along with the email

45. What does BCC stand for in email communication?

a) Blind Carbon Copy

b) Basic Communication Copy

c) Binary Content Code

d) Backward Communication Channel

Answer: - a) Blind Carbon Copy

46. What does "encryption" do in cybersecurity?

a) Translates data into a readable format

b) Protects data by converting it into an unreadable format

c) Deletes sensitive data permanently

d) Identifies system vulnerabilities

Answer: - b) Protects data by converting it into an unreadable format

47. Which of these is a type of malware?

a) Firewall

b) Antivirus

c) Ransomware

d) Router

Answer: - c) Ransomware

48. What does the term "two-factor authentication" mean?

a) Logging in with two different devices

b) Using two forms of verification for access

c) Entering the password twice

d) Using two operating systems

Answer: - b) Using two forms of verification for access

49. What is a "DDoS attack"?

a) A type of hardware failure

b) A method to block users from accessing a website

c) An attack that encrypts user data

d) A cybersecurity protocol

Answer: - b) A method to block users from accessing a website

50. What is the purpose of an antivirus program?

a) To speed up the computer

b) To remove malware from a system

c) To compress large files

d) To design secure networks

Answer: - b) To remove malware from a system

Cloud Computing

51. What is cloud computing?

a) A method of increasing internet speed

b) Storing and accessing data and programs over the internet

c) Compressing files for better storage

d) Creating secure local servers

Answer: - b) Storing and accessing data and programs over the internet

52. Which of these is an example of a cloud storage service?

a) Dropbox

b) MS Word

c) Photoshop

d) Bluetooth

Answer: - a) Dropbox

53. What does SaaS stand for?

a) Software and System

b) Secure Application as Service

c) Software as a Service

d) System Access as a Service

Answer: - c) Software as a Service

54. Which company offers the AWS (Amazon Web Services) cloud platform?

a) Google

b) Amazon

c) Microsoft

d) Apple

Answer: - b) Amazon

55. What is the main advantage of cloud computing?

a) High local storage requirements

b) Easy scalability and access from anywhere

c) Slower data retrieval

d) Reduced security

Answer: - b) Easy scalability and access from anywhere

56. What is artificial intelligence?

a) Machines performing tasks that require human intelligence

b) A type of data storage

c) A programming language

d) A type of malware

Answer: - a) Machines performing tasks that require human intelligence

57. Which of the following is a field of AI?

a) Machine Learning

b) Database Management

c) Graphic Design

d) Network Troubleshooting

Answer: - a) Machine Learning

58. What does NLP stand for in AI?

a) Neural Learning Process

b) Natural Language Processing

c) Network Link Protocol

d) New Logical Programming

Answer: - b) Natural Language Processing

59. Which is an example of AI in daily life?

a) Email spam filters

b) Using a typewriter

c) Writing a manual document

d) Turning off Wi-Fi manually

Answer: - a) Email spam filters

60. What is the term for AI systems that learn from data without being explicitly programmed?

a) Rule-based systems

b) Machine Learning

c) Static systems

d) Databasedriven systems

Answer: - b) Machine Learning

General Knowledge

61. What is the capital of Australia?

a) Sydney

b) Canberra

c) Melbourne

d) Perth

Answer: - b) Canberra

62. What is the largest planet in our solar system?

a) Earth

b) Jupiter

c) Saturn

d) Mars

Answer: - b) Jupiter

63. Which is the longest river in the world?

a) Amazon

b) Nile

c) Yangtze

d) Mississippi

Answer: - b) Nile

64. Who painted the Mona Lisa?

a) Leonardo da Vinci

b) Pablo Picasso

c) Vincent van Gogh

d) Claude Monet

Answer: - a) Leonardo da Vinci

65. What is the chemical symbol for gold?

a) Au

b) Ag

c) Fe

d) Pb

Answer: - a) Au

66. Which gas is the primary contributor to global warming?

a) Oxygen

b) Carbon Dioxide

c) Hydrogen

d) Helium

Answer: - b) Carbon Dioxide

67. What is the process by which plants make food?

a) Respiration

b) Photosynthesis

c) Combustion

d) Fermentation

Answer: - b) Photosynthesis

68. What is the main purpose of the ozone layer?

a) To cool the Earth

b) To block harmful UV radiation from the sun

c) To produce oxygen

d) To absorb water vapor

Answer: - b) To block harmful UV radiation from the sun

69. Which energy source is renewable?

a) Coal

b) Solar

c) Oil

d) Natural Gas

Answer: - b) Solar

70. What is "deforestation"?

a) Planting more trees

b) Cutting down forests

c) Building eco-friendly homes

d) Creating forest reserves

Answer: - b) Cutting down forests

Advanced General Knowledge

71. What is the smallest country in the world by land area?

a) Monaco

b) Vatican City

c) San Marino

d) Liechtenstein

Answer: - b) Vatican City

72. Who is known as the "Father of Computers"?

a) Alan Turing

b) Charles Babbage

c) John von Neumann

d) Blaise Pascal

Answer: - b) Charles Babbage

73. In which year did the Titanic sink?

a) 1912

b) 1920

c) 1905

d) 1898

Answer: - a) 1912

74. What is the hardest natural substance on Earth?

a) Gold

b) Diamond

c) Iron

d) Quartz

Answer: - b) Diamond

75. Which country invented paper?

a) India

b) China

c) Egypt

d) Greece

Answer: - b) China

History and Geography

76. Who was the first President of the United States?

a) Thomas Jefferson

b) Abraham Lincoln

c) George Washington

d) John Adams

Answer: - c) George Washington

77. Which desert is the largest in the world?

a) Gobi

b) Sahara

c) Arctic

d) Antarctic

Answer: - d) Antarctic

78. What is the name of the ancient trade route connecting China to the Mediterranean?

a) Spice Route

b) Silk Road

c) Amber Road

d) Incense Route

Answer: - b) Silk Road

79. When did World War II end?

a) 1940

b) 1945

c) 1950

d) 1939

Answer: - b) 1945

80. What is the tallest mountain in the world?

a) K2

b) Kangchenjunga

c) Mount Everest

d) Mount Kilimanjaro

Answer: - c) Mount Everest

Science and Technology

81. What is the boiling point of water at sea level in Celsius?

a) 90°C

b) 100°C

c) 120°C

d) 80°C

Answer: - b) 100°C

82. Which planet is known as the "Red Planet"?

a) Venus

b) Jupiter

c) Mars

d) Saturn

Answer: - c) Mars

83. What is the most abundant gas in Earth's atmosphere?

a) Oxygen

b) Nitrogen

c) Carbon Dioxide

d) Argon

Answer: - b) Nitrogen

84. What is the unit of electric current?

a) Volt

b) Ohm

c) Watt

d) Ampere

Answer: - d) Ampere

85. Which element has the chemical symbol "O"?

a) Oxygen

b) Osmium

c) Ozone

d) Oxide

Answer: - a) Oxygen

86. What is the full form of GDP?

a) Gross Domestic Product

b) Global Development Plan

c) General Data Processing

d) Government Development Program

Answer: - a) Gross Domestic Product

87. What does the term "inflation" mean?

a) Increase in unemployment

b) Decrease in currency value

c) Increase in the general price level of goods and services

d) Decrease in exports

Answer: - c) Increase in the general price level of goods and services

88. What is a stock market?

a) A place to buy and sell commodities

b) A marketplace to trade shares and securities

c) A savings scheme by banks

d) A place for currency exchange

Answer: - b) A marketplace to trade shares and securities

89. Which organization regulates the stock market in India?

a) RBI

b) SEBI

c) IRDA

d) NITI Aayog

Answer: - b) SEBI

90. What is the currency of Japan?

a) Yen

b) Yuan

c) Won

d) Dollar

Answer: - a) Yen

91. Which vitamin is produced in the human body when exposed to sunlight?

a) Vitamin A

b) Vitamin D

c) Vitamin C

d) Vitamin B

Answer: - b) Vitamin D

92. What is the normal body temperature in Celsius?

a) 36°C

b) 37°C

c) 38°C

d) 39°C

Answer: - b) 37°C

93. Which organ is responsible for pumping blood in the human body?

a) Lungs

b) Liver

c) Heart

d) Brain

Answer: - c) Heart

94. What is the name of the process by which the body breaks down food to release energy?

a) Respiration

b) Digestion

c) Photosynthesis

d) Metabolism

Answer: - d) Metabolism

95. Which disease is caused by a deficiency of insulin?

a) Hypertension

b) Diabetes

c) Anemia

d) Asthma

Answer: - b) Diabetes

96. Which organization is often referred to as the "World's Peacekeeper"?

a) United Nations

b) NATO

c) World Bank

d) International Red Cross

Answer: - a) United Nations

97. What does the term "democracy" mean?

a) Rule by a monarch

b) Rule by the people

c) Rule by military

d) Rule by a single party

Answer: - b) Rule by the people

98. Who was the first woman Prime Minister of India?

a) Pratibha Patil

b) Sonia Gandhi

c) Indira Gandhi

d) Sarojini Naidu

Answer: - c) Indira Gandhi

99. Where is the International Court of Justice located?

a) New York

b) Geneva

c) The Hague

d) Paris

Answer: - c) The Hague

100. Who appoints the Prime Minister in a parliamentary system of government?

a) The President

b) The Judiciary

c) The People

d) The Parliament

Answer: - a) The President

101. Who wrote the play Romeo and Juliet?

a) Charles Dickens

b) Mark Twain

c) William Shakespeare

d) George Bernard Shaw

Answer: - c) William Shakespeare

102. Which film won the first ever Academy Award for Best Picture?

a) Wings

b) Gone with the Wind

c) The Jazz Singer

d) Sunrise

Answer: - a) Wings

103. What is the national dance of Brazil?

a) Flamenco

b) Salsa

c) Samba

d) Tango

Answer: - c) Samba

104. Which instrument has 88 keys?

a) Guitar

b) Piano

c) Violin

d) Accordion

Answer: - b) Piano

105. Who is the author of The Alchemist?

a) Paulo Coelho

b) Gabriel García Márquez

c) Khaled Hosseini

d) Haruki Murakami

Answer: - a) Paulo Coelho

106. In which sport is the term "Love" used?

a) Badminton

b) Cricket

c) Tennis

d) Basketball

Answer: - c) Tennis

107. Who holds the record for the most goals scored in football history?

a) Cristiano Ronaldo

b) Lionel Messi

c) Pelé

d) Diego Maradona

Answer: - a) Cristiano Ronaldo

108. What is the length of a marathon race?

a) 21.1 km

b) 42.2 km

c) 50 km

d) 36 km

Answer: - b) 42.2 km

109. Which country has won the most FIFA World Cup titles?

a) Argentina

b) Germany

c) Brazil

d) Italy

Answer: - c) Brazil

110. In chess, which piece can only move diagonally?

a) Rook

b) Knight

c) Bishop

d) Queen

Answer: - c) Bishop

111. Which layer of the atmosphere contains the ozone layer?

a) Troposphere

b) Stratosphere

c) Mesosphere

d) Thermosphere

Answer: - b) Stratosphere

112. What is the primary cause of global warming?

a) Depletion of the ozone layer

b) Deforestation

c) Increase in greenhouse gases

d) Volcanic eruptions

Answer: - c) Increase in greenhouse gases

113. What is the process of planting trees called?

a) Afforestation

b) Deforestation

c) Agriculture

d) Cultivation

Answer: - a) Afforestation

114. Which renewable energy source uses wind to generate electricity?

a) Hydropower

b) Biomass energy

c) Wind energy

d) Solar energy

Answer: - c) Wind energy

115. What is the main source of energy for life on Earth?

a) The Moon

b) Volcanoes

c) The Sun

d) Fossil fuels

Answer: - c) The Sun

116. Which day is celebrated as International Women's Day?

a) March 8

b) April 8

c) May 8

d) June 8

Answer: - a) March 8

117. What is the name of the first artificial satellite?

a) Sputnik 1

b) Apollo 11

c) Voyager 1

d) Chandrayaan

Answer: - a) Sputnik 1

118. What does "Wi-Fi" stand for?

a) Wireless Fidelity

b) Wired Fidelity

c) Wireless Finance

d) Wireless Fiber

Answer: - a) Wireless Fidelity

119. Which zodiac sign is represented by the scales?

a) Virgo

b) Libra

c) Gemini

d) Aquarius

Answer: - b) Libra

120. What is the largest ocean in the world?

a) Atlantic Ocean

b) Indian Ocean

c) Arctic Ocean

d) Pacific Ocean

Answer: - d) Pacific Ocean

121. Which country is known as the "Land of the Rising Sun"?

a) China

b) Japan

c) South Korea

d) Thailand

Answer: - b) Japan

122. Who is the inventor of the telephone?

a) Alexander Graham Bell

b) Thomas Edison

c) Nikola Tesla

d) Guglielmo Marconi

Answer: - a) Alexander Graham Bell

123. What is the smallest planet in our solar system?

a) Mercury

b) Venus

c) Mars

d) Pluto

Answer: - a) Mercury

124. Which continent has the largest number of countries?

a) Asia

b) Africa

c) Europe

d) South America

Answer: - b) Africa

125. Who was the first man to step on the Moon?

a) Yuri Gagarin

b) Neil Armstrong

c) Buzz Aldrin

d) Michael Collins

Answer: - b) Neil Armstrong

126. What is the chemical symbol for gold?

a) Au

b) Ag

c) Pb

d) Fe

Answer: - a) Au

127. How many bones are there in the adult human body?

a) 206

b) 208

c) 210

d) 212

Answer: - a) 206

128. What is the main gas found in the air we breathe?

a) Oxygen

b) Carbon dioxide

c) Nitrogen

d) Argon

Answer: - c) Nitrogen

129. Which part of the cell is responsible for generating energy?

a) Nucleus

b) Mitochondria

c) Ribosome

d) Cell membrane

Answer: - b) Mitochondria

130. What is the unit of electrical resistance?

a) Volt

b) Ampere

c) Ohm

d) Watt

Answer: - c) Ohm

131. Who was the first President of the United States?

a) Abraham Lincoln

b) Thomas Jefferson

c) George Washington

d) John Adams

Answer: - c) George Washington

132. In which year did World War II end?

a) 1943

b) 1944

c) 1945

d) 1946

Answer: - c) 1945

133. Who was the founder of the Maurya Empire in ancient India?

a) Ashoka

b) Chandragupta Maurya

c) Bindusara

d) Kanishka

Answer: - b) Chandragupta Maurya

134. What was the name of the ship on which the Pilgrims traveled to America in 1620?

a) Titanic

b) Santa Maria

c) Mayflower

d) HMS Beagle

Answer: - c) Mayflower

135. Who is known as the “Iron Man of India”?

a) Mahatma Gandhi

b) Jawaharlal Nehru

c) Sardar Vallabhbhai Patel

d) Subhas Chandra Bose

Answer: - c) Sardar Vallabhbhai Patel

136. What does GDP stand for?

a) Gross Domestic Product

b) General Domestic Production

c) Global Domestic Product

d) Gross Distribution Profit

Answer: - a) Gross Domestic Product

137. What is the currency of Japan?

a) Yen

b) Won

c) Dollar

d) Peso

Answer: - a) Yen

138. Which organization is known for providing loans to developing countries?

a) IMF

b) WHO

c) WTO

d) UNICEF

Answer: - a) IMF

139. Who is considered the "Father of Economics"?

a) John Maynard Keynes

b) Adam Smith

c) Karl Marx

d) Alfred Marshall

Answer: - b) Adam Smith

140. What is the term for a market structure with only one seller?

a) Monopoly

b) Oligopoly

c) Perfect competition

d) Duopoly

Answer: - a) Monopoly

Geography

141. What is the capital of Canada?

a) Toronto

b) Ottawa

c) Vancouver

d) Montreal

Answer: - b) Ottawa

142. Which desert is the largest in the world?

a) Sahara

b) Gobi

c) Kalahari

d) Thar

Answer: - a) Sahara

143. Through which continent does the Amazon River flow?

a) Africa

b) Asia

c) South America

d) Australia

Answer: - c) South America

144. Mount Everest is part of which mountain range?

a) Alps

b) Andes

c) Himalayas

d) Rockies

Answer: - c) Himalayas

145. What is the longest river in the world?

a) Amazon

b) Nile

c) Yangtze

d) Mississippi

Answer: - b) Nile

146. What is the national sport of Canada?

a) Ice Hockey

b) Lacrosse

c) Basketball

d) Rugby

Answer: - b) Lacrosse

147. Which country has the most number of islands in the world?

a) Indonesia

b) Philippines

c) Sweden

d) Finland

Answer: - c) Sweden

148. What does the Roman numeral "X" represent?

a) 5

b) 10

c) 50

d) 100

Answer: - b) 10

149. Who wrote the famous novel Pride and Prejudice?

a) Charlotte Brontë

b) Emily Brontë

c) Jane Austen

d) Louisa May Alcott

Answer: - c) Jane Austen

150. Which element has the chemical symbol "O"?

a) Oxygen

b) Osmium

c) Opium

d) Ozone

Answer: - a) Oxygen

Science and Technology

151. What is the boiling point of water at sea level?

a) 90°C

b) 100°C

c) 110°C

d) 120°C

Answer: - b) 100°C

152. Which planet is known as the "Red Planet"?

a) Mars

b) Venus

c) Jupiter

d) Saturn

Answer: - a) Mars

153. Which organ in the human body is responsible for filtering blood?

a) Liver

b) Kidneys

c) Lungs

d) Heart

Answer: - b) Kidneys

154. What is the SI unit of force?

a) Newton

b) Pascal

c) Joule

d) Watt

Answer: - a) Newton

155. Which gas is most commonly used in light bulbs?

a) Argon

b) Neon

c) Helium

d) Hydrogen

Answer: - a) Argon

156. Who discovered America in 1492?

a) Vasco da Gama

b) Christopher Columbus

c) Ferdinand Magellan

d) James Cook

Answer: - b) Christopher Columbus

157. In which year was the Indian Constitution adopted?

a) 1947

b) 1948

c) 1949

d) 1950

Answer: - c) 1949

158. Who was the last Mughal emperor of India?

a) Akbar

b) Shah Jahan

c) Bahadur Shah Zafar

d) Aurangzeb

Answer: - c) Bahadur Shah Zafar

159. Where did the Industrial Revolution begin?

a) France

b) Germany

c) United States

d) United Kingdom

Answer: - d) United Kingdom

160. What was the primary cause of World War I?

a) Assassination of Archduke Franz Ferdinand

b) Treaty of Versailles

c) Pearl Harbor attack

d) Cold War tensions

Answer: - a) Assassination of Archduke Franz Ferdinand

161. Which company is known for its search engine and internet-related services?

a) Microsoft

b) Apple

c) Google

d) Amazon

Answer: - c) Google

162. What is the term for a period of economic decline?

a) Inflation

b) Recession

c) Depression

d) Stagnation

Answer: - b) Recession

163. Which of these is a cryptocurrency?

a) Litecoin

b) PayPal

c) Visa

d) MasterCard

Answer: - a) Litecoin

164. What does the abbreviation "SEZ" stand for?

a) Special Economic Zone

b) Strategic Export Zone

c) Sustainable Economic Zone

d) Social Empowerment Zone

Answer: - a) Special Economic Zone

165. Who is credited with starting the ecommerce giant Amazon?

a) Jeff Bezos

b) Elon Musk

c) Mark Zuckerberg

d) Bill Gates

Answer: - a) Jeff Bezos

166. What is the capital of Australia?

a) Sydney

b) Melbourne

c) Canberra

d) Brisbane

Answer: - c) Canberra

167. Which country is the largest in the world by area?

a) Canada

b) China

c) Russia

d) United States

Answer: - c) Russia

168. The Great Barrier Reef is located in which ocean?

a) Atlantic Ocean

b) Indian Ocean

c) Pacific Ocean

d) Southern Ocean

Answer: - c) Pacific Ocean

169. What is the smallest continent in the world?

a) Europe

b) South America

c) Australia

d) Antarctica

Answer: - c) Australia

170. Which river flows through Paris?

a) Thames

b) Seine

c) Danube

d) Rhine

Answer: - b) Seine

171. What is the largest desert in the world?

a) Arabian Desert

b) Gobi Desert

c) Sahara Desert

d) Antarctic Desert

Answer: - d) Antarctic Desert

172. Which animal is known as the "Ship of the Desert"?

a) Camel

b) Horse

c) Elephant

d) Donkey

Answer: - a) Camel

173. What is the currency of Japan?

a) Yen

b) Won

c) Yuan

d) Ringgit

Answer: - a) Yen

174. Who painted the famous artwork, Mona Lisa?

a) Michelangelo

b) Leonardo da Vinci

c) Pablo Picasso

d) Vincent van Gogh

Answer: - b) Leonardo da Vinci

175. Which is the tallest mountain in the world?

a) Mount Kilimanjaro

b) Mount Everest

c) Mount K2

d) Mount McKinley

Answer: - b) Mount Everest

176. What is the primary source of energy for the Earth?

a) Moon

b) Sun

c) Volcanoes

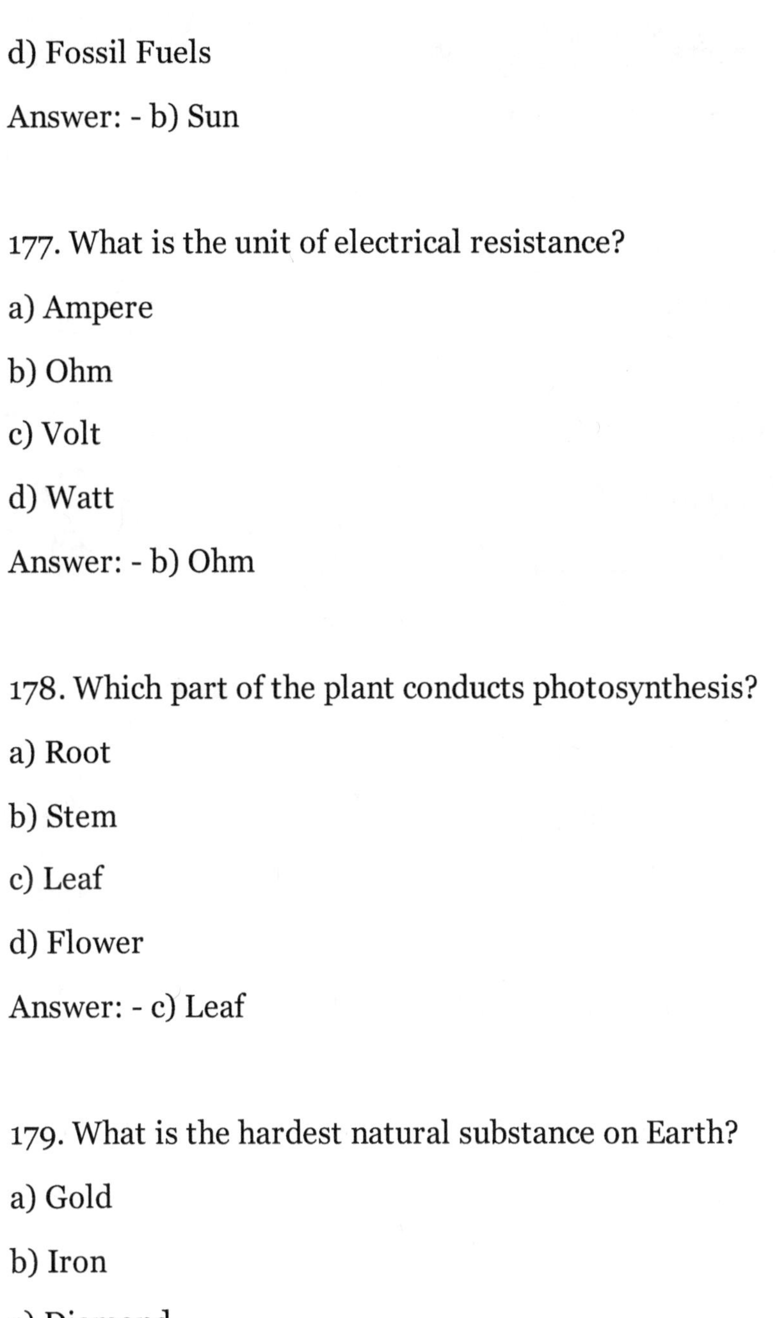

d) Fossil Fuels

Answer: - b) Sun

177. What is the unit of electrical resistance?

a) Ampere

b) Ohm

c) Volt

d) Watt

Answer: - b) Ohm

178. Which part of the plant conducts photosynthesis?

a) Root

b) Stem

c) Leaf

d) Flower

Answer: - c) Leaf

179. What is the hardest natural substance on Earth?

a) Gold

b) Iron

c) Diamond

d) Granite

Answer: - c) Diamond

180. Which is the fastest land animal?

a) Cheetah

b) Lion

c) Horse

d) Kangaroo

Answer: - a) Cheetah

181. Who was the first President of the United States?

a) Abraham Lincoln

b) George Washington

c) Thomas Jefferson

d) John Adams

Answer: - b) George Washington

182. What was the ancient Egyptian writing system called?

a) Latin

b) Cuneiform

c) Hieroglyphics

d) Sanskrit

Answer: - c) Hieroglyphics

183. In which year did World War II end?

a) 1944

b) 1945

c) 1946

d) 1947

Answer: - b) 1945

184. Who was the founder of the Maurya Empire in India?

a) Ashoka

b) Chandragupta Maurya

c) Bindusara

d) Harshavardhana

Answer: - b) Chandragupta Maurya

185. What was the first humanmade satellite to orbit Earth?

a) Explorer 1

b) Sputnik 1

c) Apollo 11

d) Voyager 1

Answer: - b) Sputnik 1

186. What does GDP stand for?

a) Gross Domestic Product

b) General Domestic Production

c) Gross Demand Pricing

d) General Data Processing

Answer: - a) Gross Domestic Product

187. Who is often referred to as the "Father of Economics"?

a) Karl Marx

b) John Maynard Keynes

c) Adam Smith

d) David Ricardo

Answer: - c) Adam Smith

188. What is the process of buying and selling goods or services using the internet called?

a) Retailing

b) Ecommerce

c) Trading

d) Marketing

Answer: - b) Ecommerce

189. Which organization regulates the monetary policy of India?

a) SEBI

b) RBI

c) NABARD

d) Finance Ministry

Answer: - b) RBI

190. What is the full form of IPO in the stock market?

a) Initial Product Offering

b) Initial Public Offering

c) International Public Offering

d) Investment Portfolio Offering

Answer: - b) Initial Public Offering

191. What is the longest river in the world?

a) Amazon

b) Nile

c) Yangtze

d) Mississippi

Answer: - b) Nile

192. Which continent is known as the “Dark Continent”?

a) Asia

b) Africa

c) South America

d) Australia

Answer: - b) Africa

193. Which ocean is the largest in the world?

a) Atlantic Ocean

b) Indian Ocean

c) Pacific Ocean

d) Arctic Ocean

Answer: - c) Pacific Ocean

194. What is the capital of South Korea?

a) Tokyo

b) Seoul

c) Bangkok

d) Jakarta

Answer: - b) Seoul

195. What is the nickname for New York City?

a) The City of Lights

b) The Big Apple

c) The Windy City

d) The Eternal City

Answer: - b) The Big Apple

196. What is the smallest country in the world by area?

a) Monaco

b) Vatican City

c) San Marino

d) Liechtenstein

Answer: - b) Vatican City

197. What does the term "COVID19" stand for?

a) Coronavirus Infectious Disease 2019

b) Common Viral Disease 2019

c) Contagious Viral Disorder 2019

d) Coronavirus Variant Disorder 2019

Answer: - a) Coronavirus Infectious Disease 2019

198. Which is the only planet in our solar system that rotates on its side?

a) Neptune

b) Venus

c) Uranus

d) Mars

Answer: - c) Uranus

199. Which country is known as the Land of the Rising Sun?

a) Japan

b) China

c) Thailand

d) South Korea

Answer: - a) Japan

200. What is the chemical symbol for gold?

a) G

b) Ag

c) Au

d) Go

Answer: - c) Au

Science and Technology

201. Which gas do plants absorb during photosynthesis?

a) Oxygen

b) Carbon Dioxide

c) Nitrogen

d) Hydrogen

Answer: - b) Carbon Dioxide

202. What is the SI unit of power?

a) Joule

b) Watt

c) Newton

d) Volt

Answer: - b) Watt

203. Who invented the telephone?

a) Thomas Edison

b) Alexander Graham Bell

c) Nikola Tesla

d) Guglielmo Marconi

Answer: - b) Alexander Graham Bell

204. Which planet is known as the "Red Planet"?

a) Venus

b) Jupiter

c) Mars

d) Mercury

Answer: - c) Mars

205. What is the primary function of white blood cells?

a) Transport oxygen

b) Fight infections

c) Digest food

d) Regulate temperature

Answer: - b) Fight infections

206. Who was the first Emperor of Rome?

a) Julius Caesar

b) Augustus

c) Nero

d) Caligula

Answer: - b) Augustus

207. When did India gain independence from British rule?

a) 1945

b) 1946

c) 1947

d) 1948

Answer: - c) 1947

208. The Great Wall of China was primarily built to protect against invasions from which group?

a) Mongols

b) Persians

c) Huns

d) Turks

Answer: - a) Mongols

209. Who discovered America in 1492?

a) Ferdinand Magellan

b) Christopher Columbus

c) Vasco da Gama

d) Amerigo Vespucci

Answer: - b) Christopher Columbus

210. Who was the first woman to win a Nobel Prize?

a) Mother Teresa

b) Rosalind Franklin

c) Marie Curie

d) Florence Nightingale

Answer: - c) Marie Curie

211. Which country has won the most FIFA World Cups?

a) Germany

b) Argentina

c) Brazil

d) Italy

Answer: - c) Brazil

212. What is the national sport of Japan?

a) Judo

b) Sumo Wrestling

c) Karate

d) Baseball

Answer: - b) Sumo Wrestling

213. Who holds the record for the most Olympic gold medals in history?

a) Michael Phelps

b) Usain Bolt

c) Carl Lewis

d) Mark Spitz

Answer: - a) Michael Phelps

214. In cricket, how many players are on the field for one team?

a) 9

b) 10

c) 11

d) 12

Answer: - c) 11

215. What is the diameter of a standard basketball hoop in inches?

a) 15 inches

b) 18 inches

c) 20 inches

d) 22 inches

Answer: - b) 18 inches

216. What is the capital of Canada?

a) Toronto

b) Ottawa

c) Vancouver

d) Montreal

Answer: - b) Ottawa

217. Which river flows through Paris?

a) Rhine

b) Thames

c) Seine

d) Danube

Answer: - c) Seine

218. What is the smallest ocean in the world?

a) Atlantic Ocean

b) Arctic Ocean

c) Indian Ocean

d) Pacific Ocean

Answer: - b) Arctic Ocean

219. Which desert is the hottest in the world?

a) Sahara Desert

b) Arabian Desert

c) Atacama Desert

d) Kalahari Desert

Answer: - a) Sahara Desert

220. What is the official language of Brazil?

a) Spanish

b) Portuguese

c) French

d) English

Answer: - b) Portuguese

221. Who wrote "Romeo and Juliet"?

a) Charles Dickens

b) Jane Austen

c) William Shakespeare

d) Mark Twain

Answer: - c) William Shakespeare

222. Which novel begins with the line "Call me Ishmael"?

a) Moby Dick

b) The Great Gatsby

c) Pride and Prejudice

d) To Kill a Mockingbird

Answer: - a) Moby Dick

223. Who is the author of the Harry Potter series?

a) J.R.R. Tolkien

b) Suzanne Collins

c) J.K. Rowling

d) George R.R. Martin

Answer: - c) J.K. Rowling

224. What is the title of the first book in the "Lord of the Rings" trilogy?

a) The Hobbit

b) The Fellowship of the Ring

c) The Two Towers

d) The Return of the King

Answer: - b) The Fellowship of the Ring

225. In which book would you find the character "Atticus Finch"?

a) The Catcher in the Rye

b) Moby Dick

c) To Kill a Mockingbird

d) 1984

Answer: - c) To Kill a Mockingbird

226. Who painted the Mona Lisa?

a) Vincent van Gogh

b) Pablo Picasso

c) Leonardo da Vinci

d) Claude Monet

Answer: - c) Leonardo da Vinci

227. Which famous composer wrote "The Four Seasons"?

a) Ludwig van Beethoven

b) Wolfgang Amadeus Mozart

c) Antonio Vivaldi

d) Johann Sebastian Bach

Answer: - c) Antonio Vivaldi

228. What is the national anthem of the United States called?

a) America the Beautiful

b) God Bless America

c) The Star Spangled Banner

d) My Country, 'Tis of Thee

Answer: - c) The Star Spangled Banner

229. Which artist is known for the work "The Persistence of Memory"?

a) Salvador Dalí

b) Andy Warhol

c) Henri Matisse

d) Pablo Picasso

Answer: - a) Salvador Dalí

230. Which instrument is known as the "king of instruments"?

a) Violin

b) Piano

c) Organ

d) Guitar

Answer: - c) Organ

231. What does GDP stand for?

a) Gross Domestic Product

b) General Domestic Product

c) Global Domestic Price

d) Government Debt Percentage

Answer: - a) Gross Domestic Product

232. Which is the largest stock exchange in the world by market capitalization?

a) Tokyo Stock Exchange

b) London Stock Exchange

c) Shanghai Stock Exchange

d) New York Stock Exchange

Answer: - d) New York Stock Exchange

233. What is the main purpose of the World Bank?

a) To lend money to governments for military spending

b) To provide loans for economic development

c) To offer grants for environmental projects

d) To invest in the stock market

Answer: - b) To provide loans for economic development

234. Which currency is used in Japan?

a) Yen

b) Dollar

c) Euro

d) Won

Answer: - a) Yen

235. What is inflation?

a) Decrease in the general price level of goods and services

b) Increase in the general price level of goods and services

c) The rate at which people save money

d) The change in consumer demand

Answer: - b) Increase in the general price level of goods and services

Technology and Innovations

236. Who is the cofounder of Microsoft?

a) Steve Jobs

b) Bill Gates

c) Larry Page

d) Mark Zuckerberg

Answer: - b) Bill Gates

237. What year was the first iPhone released?

a) 2005

b) 2006

c) 2007

d) 2008

Answer: - c) 2007

238. What does "HTTP" stand for in a website URL?

a) HyperText Transfer Protocol

b) HighTech Transfer Protocol

c) HyperTransfer Technology Protocol

d) Hyperlink Transfer Text Protocol

Answer: - a) HyperText Transfer Protocol

239. Which company developed the first successful personal computer?

a) Microsoft

b) Apple

c) IBM

d) Hewlett-Packard

Answer: - b) Apple

240. What is the name of the first artificial Earth satellite?

a) Sputnik 1

b) Apollo 11

c) Voyager 1

d) Hubble

Answer: - a) Sputnik 1

241. Who is known as the father of modern medicine?

a) Hippocrates

b) Galen

c) William Harvey

d) Avicenna

Answer: - a) Hippocrates

242. What is the main function of red blood cells?

a) Fight infections

b) Carry oxygen

c) Produce antibodies

d) Aid in digestion

Answer: - b) Carry oxygen

243. Which vitamin is primarily obtained from sunlight?

a) Vitamin A

b) Vitamin B12

c) Vitamin C

d) Vitamin D

Answer: - d) Vitamin D

244. What is the medical term for high blood pressure?

a) Hyperglycemia

b) Hypertension

c) Hypotension

d) Hyperlipidemia

Answer: - b) Hypertension

245. What is the largest organ in the human body?

a) Heart

b) Brain

c) Liver

d) Skin

Answer: - d) Skin

246. Who was the first president of the United States?

a) Thomas Jefferson

b) Abraham Lincoln

c) George Washington

d) John Adams

Answer: - c) George Washington

247. In which year did World War I begin?

a) 1912

b) 1914

c) 1916

d) 1918

Answer: - b) 1914

248. Who discovered America in 1492?

a) Ferdinand Magellan

b) Christopher Columbus

c) Marco Polo

d) Leif Erikson

Answer: - b) Christopher Columbus

249. What ancient civilization built the pyramids in Egypt?

a) Roman

b) Greek

c) Egyptian

d) Mayan

Answer: - c) Egyptian

250. Who was the first emperor of China?

a) Liu Bang

b) Qin Shi Huang

c) Sun Tzu

d) Cao Cao

Answer: - b) Qin Shi Huang

Geography

251. What is the capital city of France?

a) Berlin

b) Paris

c) Rome

d) Madrid

Answer: - b) Paris

252. Which river is the longest in the world?

a) Amazon

b) Nile

c) Yangtze

d) Mississippi

Answer: - b) Nile

253. Mount Everest is located in which mountain range?

a) Andes

b) Alps

c) Himalayas

d) Rockies

Answer: - c) Himalayas

254. What is the largest desert in the world?

a) Sahara

b) Gobi

c) Kalahari

d) Antarctic Desert

Answer: - d) Antarctic Desert

255. Which country has the largest population in the world?

a) India

b) United States

c) China

d) Indonesia

Answer: - c) China

256. How many players are on a standard football (soccer) team?

a) 9

b) 10

c) 11

d) 12

Answer: - c) 11

257. Which country hosted the 2016 Summer Olympics?

a) China

b) United States

c) Brazil

d) Russia

Answer: - c) Brazil

258. Who holds the record for the most goals scored in World Cup history?

a) Cristiano Ronaldo

b) Lionel Messi

c) Pele

d) Miroslav Klose

Answer: - d) Miroslav Klose

259. What sport is known as "the king of sports"?

a) Baseball

b) Basketball

c) Soccer

d) Tennis

Answer: - c) Soccer

260. Who won the first ever Formula 1 World Championship in 1950?

a) Juan Manuel Fangio

b) Stirling Moss

c) Alberto Ascari

d) Giuseppe Farina

Answer: - d) Giuseppe Farina

261. Who is known as the father of the computer?

a) Charles Babbage

b) Alan Turing

c) Bill Gates

d) Steve Jobs

Answer: - a) Charles Babbage

262. What year was the first iPhone released?

a) 2005

b) 2007

c) 2009

d) 2010

Answer: - b) 2007

263. What does "HTTP" stand for in a website address?

a) Hyper Transfer Text Protocol

b) Hyper Text Transfer Protocol

c) Hyper Terminal Transfer Protocol

d) High Traffic Text Protocol

Answer: - b) Hyper Text Transfer Protocol

264. Who invented the first practical telephone?

a) Thomas Edison

b) Alexander Graham Bell

c) Nikola Tesla

d) Samuel Morse

Answer: - b) Alexander Graham Bell

265. Which company developed the Windows operating system?

a) Apple

b) Google

c) Microsoft

d) IBM

Answer: - c) Microsoft

266. Who played the character of Jack Dawson in the movie Titanic?

a) Leonardo DiCaprio

b) Brad Pitt

c) Matt Damon

d) Johnny Depp

Answer: - a) Leonardo DiCaprio

267. What is the name of the fictional wizarding school in Harry Potter?

a) Durmstrang

b) Beauxbatons

c) Hogwarts

d) Ilvermorny

Answer: - c) Hogwarts

268. Who directed the movie Jurassic Park?

a) Steven Spielberg

b) James Cameron

c) Martin Scorsese

d) George Lucas

Answer: - a) Steven Spielberg

269. In which year was the first Star Wars film released?

a) 1973

b) 1975

c) 1977

d) 1980

Answer: - c) 1977

270. Which animated movie features the song "Let It Go"?

a) Moana

b) Frozen

c) Tangled

d) Mulan

Answer: - b) Frozen

271. Who wrote Romeo and Juliet?

a) Charles Dickens

b) William Shakespeare

c) Jane Austen

d) Mark Twain

Answer: - b) William Shakespeare

272. Which novel begins with the line, "Call me Ishmael"?

a) MobyDick

b) The Great Gatsby

c) Crime and Punishment

d) To Kill a Mockingbird

Answer: - a) MobyDick

273. What is the title of the first Harry Potter book?

a) Harry Potter and the Goblet of Fire

b) Harry Potter and the Philosopher's Stone

c) Harry Potter and the Chamber of Secrets

d) Harry Potter and the Prisoner of Azkaban

Answer: - b) Harry Potter and the Philosopher's Stone

274. Who wrote 1984?

a) Aldous Huxley

b) George Orwell

c) J.R.R. Tolkien

d) Ray Bradbury

Answer: - b) George Orwell

275. What is the fictional land where The Chronicles of Narnia takes place?

a) Middle Earth

b) Narnia

c) Oz

d) Wonderland

Answer: - b) Narnia

276. Who painted the Mona Lisa?

a) Vincent van Gogh

b) Claude Monet

c) Pablo Picasso

d) Leonardo da Vinci

Answer: - d) Leonardo da Vinci

277. What is the name of the famous sculpture by Michelangelo depicting a young David?

a) The Thinker

b) David

c) The Pietà

d) Venus de Milo

Answer: - b) David

278. In which city is the famous museum, the Louvre, located?

a) New York

b) London

c) Paris

d) Rome

Answer: - c) Paris

279. Who is the artist behind the painting The Starry Night?

a) Claude Monet

b) Pablo Picasso

c) Vincent van Gogh

d) Edvard Munch

Answer: - c) Vincent van Gogh

280. Which art movement is Pablo Picasso most associated with?

a) Impressionism

b) Surrealism

c) Cubism

d) Baroque

Answer: - c) Cubism

281. Which is the largest continent by land area?

a) Africa

b) Asia

c) Europe

d) North America

Answer: - b) Asia

282. What is the capital city of Canada?

a) Toronto

b) Montreal

c) Ottawa

d) Vancouver

Answer: - c) Ottawa

283. Which country has the longest coastline in the world?

a) United States

b) Russia

c) Canada

d) Australia

Answer: - c) Canada

284. Which river is the longest in the world?

a) Amazon River

b) Nile River

c) Yangtze River

d) Mississippi River

Answer: - b) Nile River

285. Which desert is the largest in the world?

a) Sahara Desert

b) Arabian Desert

c) Gobi Desert

d) Kalahari Desert

Answer: - a) Sahara Desert

286. Who was the first President of the United States?

a) Thomas Jefferson

b) Abraham Lincoln

c) George Washington

d) John Adams

Answer: - c) George Washington

287. Which empire was ruled by Julius Caesar?

a) Ottoman Empire

b) Roman Empire

c) Byzantine Empire

d) British Empire

Answer: - b) Roman Empire

288. In which year did the Titanic sink?

a) 1902

b) 1912

c) 1922

d) 1932

Answer: - b) 1912

289. The Battle of Hastings in 1066 was fought in which country?

a) France

b) Germany

c) England

d) Italy

Answer: - c) England

290. Who was the first woman to fly solo across the Atlantic Ocean?

a) Amelia Earhart

b) Bessie Coleman

c) Jacqueline Cochran

d) Harriet Quimby

Answer: - a) Amelia Earhart

291. Which country won the first FIFA World Cup in 1930?

a) Argentina

b) Brazil

c) Germany

d) Uruguay

Answer: - d) Uruguay

292. How many players are there on a standard football (soccer) team?

a) 9

b) 10

c) 11

d) 12

Answer: - c) 11

293. Who holds the record for the most Olympic gold medals?

a) Usain Bolt

b) Michael Phelps

c) Simone Biles

d) Carl Lewis

Answer: - b) Michael Phelps

294. Which sport is known as the "king of sports"?

a) Football

b) Cricket

c) Tennis

d) Basketball

Answer: - a) Football

295. In which sport would you perform a slam dunk?

a) Tennis

b) Football

c) Basketball

d) Volleyball

Answer: - c) Basketball

296. What is the chemical symbol for gold?

a) Au

b) Ag

c) Pb

d) Fe

Answer: - a) Au

297. What is the process by which plants make their food?

a) Respiration

b) Digestion

c) Photosynthesis

d) Absorption

Answer: - c) Photosynthesis

298. Who developed the theory of relativity?

a) Isaac Newton

b) Albert Einstein

c) Nikola Tesla

d) Galileo Galilei

Answer: - b) Albert Einstein

299. What is the most common gas in the Earth's atmosphere?

a) Oxygen

b) Nitrogen

c) Carbon Dioxide

d) Hydrogen

Answer: - b) Nitrogen

300. What is the hardest natural substance on Earth?

a) Gold

b) Diamond

c) Iron

d) Platinum

Answer: - b) Diamond

www.ingramcontent.com/pod-product-compliance
Lightning Source LLC
LaVergne TN
LVHW051347050326
832903LV00030B/2891

* 9 7 9 8 3 0 4 3 4 6 8 6 3 *